# Closing the Gap

## Computer Development in the People's Republic of China

# Closing the Gap

## Computer Development in the People's Republic of China

EDITED BY

## Otto W. Witzell and J.K. Lee Smith

**Westview Press**
BOULDER, SAN FRANCISCO, & LONDON

*Westview Special Studies in Science, Technology, and Public Policy*

Copyright © 1989 by Westview Press, Inc.

Published in 1989 in the United States of America by Westview Press, Inc., 5500 Central Avenue, Boulder, Colorado 80301, and in the United Kingdom by Westview Press, Inc., 13 Brunswick Centre, London WC1N 1AF, England

Library of Congress Cataloging-in-Publication Data
Witzell, Otto W.
    Closing the gap : computer development in the People's Republic of
China / by Otto W. Witzell and J.K. Lee Smith.
        p.   cm.—(Westview special studies in science, technology,
and public policy)
    Bibliography: p.
    Includes index.
    ISBN 0-8133-7692-0
1. Computer Industry—China.  2. Computers—China.  I. Lee Smith,
J.K.  II. Title.  III. Series.
HD9696.C63C68   1989
338.4'7004'0951—dc19                                                       88-27768
                                                                              CIP

Printed and bound in the United States of America

(∞)  The paper used in this publication meets the requirements of the American National Standard for
      Permanence of Paper for Printed Library Materials Z39.48-1984.

10    9    8    7    6    5    4    3    2    1

# CONTENTS

# TABLES AND FIGURES

# I. ASSESSMENT OF CHINA'S COMPUTER CAPABILITY

## CHARACTERISTICS OF THE OVERALL COMPUTER STRUCTURE

### Organization, Structure and Function

Simplisitically, from the Chinese point of view, their computer world is structured in four parts: 1) research and development; 2) manufacturing and service; 3) application and popularization; and 4) education and training. In actuality, viewed from the perspective of 1988, it is a comprehensive, complicated, cumbersome, sometimes overlapping, and changing structure. It is truly a many splendored apparatus. It is possible to view this apparatus or structure as having at least ten parts:

* A government substructure
* A research and development substructure
* A manufacturing substucture
* A maintenance and service substructure
* A trade import and export substructure
* An end user or functional substructure
* The professional society substructure
* A military substructure

### Complexity and Vertical Integration

Certainly the overall structure is a complex one. On many occasions the impact of vertical integration is overriding in isolating one structure from another. For example, the Chinese Academy of Sciences computer units have tended to not interact with the computer units of the Ministry of Electronics Industry. (2)   Although there are numerous reports of units collaborating in the development of a piece of equipment, these interactions tend to be characterized by interactions

1

between factories of one ministry and universities doing business with that ministry and/or local provincial or municipal units. Recently, MEI has decentralized to the extent of extending local partial autonomy to many of its units. It is apparent, however, that the structure still contains and maintains competing elements rather than cooperating units.

Between 1990 and 2000 when the sophistication capability of personnel is expected to reach full maturity, a severe price may be paid for the quasi-isolation induced by the emphasis on vertical integration unless efforts are made to bring about effective cooperation. What the Chinese would miss is the added increment of progress which can be achieved by multidisciplinary teams being pulled together from a variety of organizations.

There is evidence that the Chinese are attempting to correct the situation. In February 1987, the State Council issued a set of regulations to provide integration of scientific and technological research and industrial production. Efforts involving such cooperation include six research institutes of CAS working together with enterprises as a unit. The unit will have one scientific, production, marketing and accounting system. Another such cooperative arrangement includes a group of plants under MEI which will fund an electrical circuits lab at Qinghua University. It is expected that this will reduce duplication of research and provide the plants with access to advanced technology. (188) Fudan and some other leading universities have been assembling multidisciplinary efforts. These efforts are only a start and it remains to be seen what the eventual results will be. As the level of competency of S&T personnel gets better, the potential loss that can result from isolation of related competencies found in different structures due to vertical integration can become important. The most serious impact would occur at the moment when China is ready to make an effort to close the gap between itself and the leading edge of the computer world. If the changes to promote interaction are effective, China will be optimizing the use of its personnel resources so that they can collectively and cooperatively give far more in interaction than isolation.


Personnel Character and Policy

Generally, the S&T hierarchy consists of older intellectuals, some of whom were trained abroad. Most were trained prior to 1950 or between 1950 and 1960.(1) The computer hierarchy has some similar characteristics. Many could speak English, had been trained in the U.S., and had a bias in favor of U.S. computer equipment.(2) However, since 1985 there is considerable evidence of a youth movement in the Academy of Sciences and the Ministry of Electronics Industry.

Personnel characteristics have had something to do with the major policy decisions to accept help from such organizations as the United Nations, the World Bank and to use the joint venture mechanism. This policy decision has resulted from the accurate perception of an informed hierarchy -- a hierarchy that saw the computer world outside of China exploding, and concluded that its first priorites must be to access now, the best equipment possible, to develop its own computer production base and technical manpower base as rapidly as possible while importing as much technology as feasible. This strategy is aimed at getting China in a position to close the computer gap between itself and the rest of the world between 1990 and 2000.

## Dynamics and Growth

During the late seventies and through 1986, the overall structure had been developing rapidly with the emergence of provincial and municipal computer centers, service centers, user organizations, new computer departments at universities, new computer professional societies and more computer and components factories. All of these structures were attempting to address problems and respond to national needs. The expansion of the total structure clearly was intended to sustain rapid expansion of the total computer effort.

The China computerworld continues to be in an experimental transition phase. One of the most prominent of the ongoing reforms has been the creation of The Leading Group for the Invigoration of the Electronics Industry by the State Council in 1984. The subordinate organization which has the greatest substantive responsibility for China's overall electronics and computer development strategy is the Office of the Leading Group for Electronics. This office is divided into four functional subgroups most of whom have advisory groups. The groups include computers, ICs, applications and software and a communications group.

However, expansion brought with it growing pains and a variety of problems such as:

* the need to increase the output of technically trained personnel
* the need for quality control in the manufacturing process in factories
* prioritizing assignment to control competition for quality personnel
* the need to improve up time and utilization of computers in service
* the need to improve the return on investment in their computer world

China has attempted to address the problem of increasing the output of technically trained manpower by expanding the level of vocational and technical training and by increasing the university input from five percent to thirteen percent of middle school graduates. Competition for personnel seemingly is controlled by the somewhat mysterious Bureau of Science and Technology Personnel (BSTP) of the State Science and Technology

Commission, and the market place.

There is recognition of the need to get quality personnel in the factories, but the fact that the universities and the academies up to 1985 continued to keep their best products for themselves gave no evidence of a decision for a course of action to bring about an increase in the quality of personnel to be found in the manufacturing process. In 1985 in Changsha and in 1986 in Shanghai however, it was possible to identify some better trained personnel in factory management.(130)

In response to the need for product quality control, China has established a high level standards group in the computer area. This is an important step which can impact uniform production, improved machinery, compatibility of software and reduce maintenance.

China's growing sensitivity to the importance of standards is also evidenced by both the emergence of a nongovernmental private association for the standardization of computers and its participation in the International Standardization Organization. The Institute of Scientific and Technical Information, ISTIC, has represented China at these meetings. The problem of standards gets involved with compatibility of mainframes, peripherals, and software. China has recognized this problem and is addressing it from both the point of view of improved manufacture and a service structure. As a consequence, they are attempting to improve both quality and productivity as well as return on investment. Although the setting of standards is an important step, it does not insure quality products. In this sense great achievments are yet to be seen.

An awareness of the signifigance of data bases is represented by the stated mission of the Yan Shan S&T Corporation of the Chinese Academy of Social Sciences and the Institute of Scientific and Technical Information (ISTIC) of the State Science and Technology Commission. The UN census computer effort and its support of the International Economic Information Processing and Training Center is also an indicator of progress. Another specific example was the development of China's first carbon spectral nuclear magnetic resonance data bank by six scientists from Henan.(4)

Another important goal connected with the dynamics of the system or structure, is networking. In 1981 the network system was reported in a preliminary state.(5) However, in 1980, there had been a report of the first cooperative network for computerized medical use software.(6) In 1982, there was a report of a computer network being built which uses a large imported computer as the central machine. This project had been proposed after two years of network building experiments.(7) Confirmation of network planning was obtained in September, 1982 during discussions with computer people at Jiaotung Xian University, and Northwest Polytechnic also in Xian. Their network effort was reported as being part of a five-year plan with the intention of netting within a university as the first step, netting among universities as step two, and netting regionally as step three. The problem of construction of such a net was discussed in terms of new dedicated lines and new switch gear on an as needed basis.(2) By 1985 a great deal of attention was being paid to the problem of networking. However, experimentation tended to be on a localized basis and was usually carried out with micros. The real obstacle to progress continues to be the telecommunication system. The 1986 baud rate ranged from a low of 50 to a high of 250. Long distance computer telecommunications under these conditions is impossible. The lack of effective computer networks is still a serious deterrent to the rapid development of profitable business. There are still serious impediments to the travelers ability to schedule train, plane, and hotel reservations. Until a combination of new long lines, new modern switchgear, microwave stations in quantity, and satellite links are available, no effective networking will appear.(130) Upgrading of the system is being planned in Tianjin Beijing and Shanghai. Belgians, French, Japanese and Swedes are to be engaged in this work. Our assessment is that improvement in wired computer telecommunications is at least five years away. Even then it will be limited to the environs of a few large cities. Microwave stations are to be seen but their availability for computer networking is severely limited. Countrywide availability of effective computer telecommunications may be as much as ten years away.

Several steps in improving the communication system have occured. First, China completed 960 and 600 channel microwave networks connecting Beijing, the provinces, Tianjin and Shanghai but excluding the autonomous regions of the Nei Mongol and Xizang. In addtion,they completed an 1800 channel coaxial route connecting Shenyang and Guangzhou via Beijing, Tianjin, Jinan, Shanghai and Hangzhou. Depending on the proximity of a potential user to the cable, computer networking might be realized. There was also the execution of an agreement by the Essex Group of the United Technologies Corporation (USA) and various Chinese corporations involving the Chengdu Cable Plant. This plant has been revamped to manufacture polyolefine insulated integral sheathed telephone cable.(8)

Another somewhat related example of a program in this area is the installation in 1980 of the Hong Kong S&T computer terminal search equipment at the China Overseas Construction Engineering Company which has the capability of maintaining contact through international communication satellites with Lockheed and the System Development Corporation of the U.S.(9) What is important here is the potential for access to the dialog system.

By 1988 three high speed digital telecommunications circuits connected Beijing to Shanghai, Chengdu, Wuhan and Guangzhou for meteorological communications using microcomputers.

Production and Imports

A conservative estimate of China's annual production of large, medium and small computers in 1980 would be about one to two hundred.

By 1982 very significant increases started to occur according to Li Rui, then head of the State Administration for Computer Industry (SACI) now known as the Administration of Computer Industry (ACI). He indicated in October 1982 that China was capable of producing 500 large, medium, and small size computers as well as 500 micros annually. He also indicated that there was a 62% increase in large, medium, and small computers and a 160% increase in micros. However, in analysis of his report, China apparently produced an extra 160 large, medium, and small sized computers between January and September of 1982, which was an increase of 62% over the corresponding period of the previous year.(10) It is possible that Li Rui was overstating in spite of supporting data from China Reconstructs.(11)

Li Rui's goals were ambitious:

*1985 annual production of 1000 large, medium and small
   computers and 10,000 micros and single board computers
* 1990 annual production of 1800 large, medium and
   small computers, and 40,000 micros and single board computers

As early as 1982 the stage was set for the future start of serial production of 30 large scale integrated circuit lines . This was an important step in the direction of being able to produce more computers domestically. The development of these lines was the result of a nationwide research program on production techniques.(16) This would tend to support the achievement of Li Rui's goals. By 1983 the target of 2700 micros was exceeded with an annual production of 5436 machines. In addition 364 mainframes and minis were produced.(160) It was reported in 1985 that the total output of computers in 1984 was estimated to be approximately 600% more than in 1983. This includes the reported annual production capacity of over 10,000 units of the Great Wall and 10,000 of the Zijin II.(164)

Tax incentives supportive of Li Rui's goals were reported in 1986. These incentives are available to research institutes if they spend their tax savings on further R & D. Exemptions on business taxes and income taxes are available on earnings from services, exports, and technology transfer, as are reductions on product and value added taxes on new products.(144) Domestic production has been complemented by the outreach moves of the overall structures. This has been underscored in reporting on joint venture computer production efforts particularly involving France, the US and Japan. Also the United Nations has been responsible for approximately thirty computers from companies such as Burroughs, Hewlitt-Packard, and IBM being put in place in China. In addition the World Bank in phase I was responsible for fourteen Honeywell machines being placed. Approximately fifty large computers is close to ten percent of what China has imported. The Chinese probably feel by now that the UN and World Bank transactions are expeditious and allow for more powerful machines. Thus, the import structure, in spite of complexity, corruption, turbulence and other problems has functioned fairly well. In fact, it has functioned so well that it was reported that China had imported 600 standard computers and approximately 100,000 micros and single boards from fourteen countries at an approximate cost of $500 million. If one looks ahead, the prospects appear even brighter on imports.(10,12,165) In 1985 two private communications indicated that China had spent $300 million to acquire foreign micros during 1984.

Some of the significant orders reported by various issues of the China Business Review and the Japanese Economic Journal since 1982 include:

United States

Wang
One 32 bit VS100 mini system for CAS
Fifteen 2200 LVP systems for State Bureau of Supplies
One VS50 system for China North Industry Company
Two VS80 systems for People's Bank of Guangdong
Prime and Seed Hong Kong Ltd.
U.N. award of computer monitoring system for Yellow River Basin
Honeywell Information and World Bank
Fourteen DPS8s for Chinese universities
Honeywell Inc. and Great Wall Industrial Co.
DPS 6 small computer systems.
Eagle Computer Inc.
PC+ and PC+ XL desk top computers
Sage Computer and Data Medium Hong Kong
One hundred Sage IV and two hundred Basis Medfly micro systems.
Control Data Corp.and Nuclear Energy Institute, CAS
Two Cyber-825s,
Control Data Corp. and Shanghai Power Energy
Research Inst.
One Cyber-830 for development of nuclear energy program.
Digital Equipment Co. and Automated Systems, Hong Kong
Three VAX 11/750 minis for universities
Digital Equipment Co. and Ministry of Water Conservancy and Power
Four VAX 11/780 minis for power design and planning and hydro design
Hewlitt Packard
Fourteen HP 3000 systems
Perkin Elmer and Central Iron and Steel Inst.
One 3252 XP machine for research
One 3205 for process control
Two 7350/A super micros

GE Calma,  and Ministry of Water Resources  and
Electric Power
    Sixty CAD systems for process control and design
Greyhound Computer Corp. and Cometals Inc.
    Refurbished IBM computers


Japan


Nine DG MV6000 for Mington New Technical
Development Corp.(13)
NEC, Sumitomo Shoji Kaisha and INSTRIMPEX
    305 micros for education and science
Sord Computer Corp. and  CASS
    30 to 40 computer systems
Sanyo Electric Co.
    1000 micros.
Hitachi and People's Bank of China
    M 240H large scale general purpose  computers
    M 240D medium scale general purpose  computers
    M 220D medium scale general purpose  computers
    L 470X  small scale general purpose  computers and
        terminals

The prospects for increased computer acquisition were good. The National
Council on U.S. China Trade reported in 1983, that the Chinese might
double or triple imports of U.S. computers aided by their then growing
favorable trade balance and mounting hard currency reserves.(20)  Such
imports did in fact take place. Record trade surplus put China in its
strongest financial position ever. Foreign exchange reserves were projected
to reach $8 billion by the end of 1982.(14)  By the end of 1984 foreign
exchange reserves reached $17 billion. Transactions such as the sale by
Beijing Computing Technology Institute of 1000 BVM111 single board
micros to West Germany have helped.(15) Recently, the situation has
changed, however, and foreign exchange levels have declined and China
began closing the doors to US and Japanese computer makers. Various US
companies were reported as feeling the squeeze.(150) The short term
market, therefore, appears to be much weaker.


Summary

    The structure is vital, it is expanding and responding to problems,
some more vigorously than others. Probably the most serious problems are
redundancy elimination, optimization of resource allocation, manpower
shortage, peripherals, precision machining, network limitations, and
standards. These problems represent areas where response has not
occurred, is just starting, or has not achieved as much as in other fields

such as plant development, start up of serial and mass production, software, the elimination of the shortage of foreign exchange and the development of relationships with the UN and World Bank.

Probably the two areas of manpower and manufacturing should be singled out because of their great immediate importance. Manpower is a very serious problem because it is being stretched like a rubber band to hold together the rapidly expanding computer structure. Many of the technical and scientific persons working in the computer area are much older persons who obtained their training abroad and returned to China in the 1950s. However, computer developments worldwide had not really gotten very far until the 50s and 60s. Compounding the problem was the Cultural Revolution (a lost decade) and the consequent disruption of the higher education system with the result that many of the key personnel in the forefront of computer developments have not recieved any systematic training for many years.(17,18) The personnel shortage is further complicated because of China's isolation from the rest of the world for a long period. This point of view is supported by the fact that the director of the Institute of Software R&D, CAS asked for help in obtaining additional training for three of his older key personnel.

Manufacturing is a very serious problem because of the lack of progress in serial and mass production and the fundamental issue of lack of precise machine production.

Certainly the overall complex structure had received centralized direction and encouragement from above. A small cadre still does know what is going on. Somehow there has been reasonable coordination between the State Council, The Leading Group for the Invigoration of the Electronics Industry, the State Planning Commission, the State Economic Commission and the State Science and Technology Commission. There are indications that some decentralization is taking place. It is estimated by Simon and Rhen, (68) that by the end of 1986 approximately 10% of MEIs key enterprises will remain under its control with most of these engaged in defense oriented work. MEIs Administration of Computer Industry (ACI) will supervise only nine computer manufacturing organizations, four service corporations, two development centers and three computer user associations.(164) Consistent with this is the situation in Shanghai where the key enterprises in the electronic and computer industries fall directly under the control of local authorities. During a November 1986 visit, the authors were told by the Deputy Chief Engineer of the Shanghai Electronic Computer Factory that it gets most of its funding from the municipal government and receives only technical guidance from MEI. This factory is part of the Shanghai Computer Corporation. However, the mechanisms and procedures are elusive. Their presence can only be deduced because of the achievment of good results as for example the development of four generations of computers, and the continuity of effort and program from the late 70s through the 80s. Examples of this are:

* In January 1982, the PRC put into operation an automated
    meteorological data processing and interchange system using
    three large size Japanese computers to automatically
    process and interchange nationwide meteorological data with the
    National Beijing Center. Wire speed for transmission was
    50 baud.(19)
* The 960 and 600 channel microwave networks and the 1800
    channel coaxial cable, all of which establish long range potential
    for networking.(19)
* The establisment of a profit making Beijing Associates Software
    Development Association is underway. It will develop, design,
    maintain and transplant programs for domestic and foreign
    customers on a contracted basis as well as provide consulting
    and training.(54)
* In 1985 two new organizations were identified. They were the
    China Software Technique Corporation, MEI and the Institute
    of Software R&D of CAS.(130)
* The Computer Application Institute of MEI was renamed The
    Research Institute of Computer System Engineering in 1985.
* Development of HZ82 intelligent Chinese terminals displaying
    Chinese characters at high speed.
* Development of data base RTDB-130 which is a business
    network DBMS and seventy other data base systems, nearly
    half of which have been developed by the Chinese.(13)
* Recent computers have achieved operating speeds of 10 mops for
    the CAS's 757 and 100 mops for the Galaxy.
* The reported annual production level for China in 1982 was 500
    large, medium and small computers and 500 micros.This
    reflects a dramatic increase in production in the first eight to
    nine months of 1982 as contrasted to the same period in 1981.
* By 1986 the PRC had also achieved an approximate inventory of
    7000 computers, not including micros.
* The production capability and the inventory will be substantially
    augmented in the future as a result of the growing number of
    cooperative and joint venture agreements
* Even though one report indicates 500 computercenters
    throughout the country, (21) the bulk of the computer structure
    is located between Harbin in the north, Guangzhou in the south,
    and Shaanxi province in the west, with major competitive
    concentrations in the Beijing area, the greater Shanghai area and
    Guangzhou. Wide geographic distribution has occurred, which
    has given China an insurance policy for self reliance.

In 1978, Fang Yi outlined objectives which included production of
large scale ICs, development of the technology for ultra-large scale ICs,
turning out giant computers, obtaining serial production of a range of
computers, and developing peripherals, software, applied mathematics

and applications for computers. The objectives are being worked on but the structure is suffering from growing pains and cannot accomplish everything at once. In regard to China's isolation from the cutting edge of the computer world, and its decision to reach out using the UN and the World Bank, it is important to note that on April 14, 1982 Basic Computer Science found its way into the Chinese Academy of Sciences, and the National Science Foundation Cooperative Research Protocols.

## DOMESTIC COMPUTERS AND THEIR CAPABILITIES

### Hardware

Chinese efforts to develop a domestic computer capability began in the late 1950s. Their early efforts were supported by a heavy influx of Russian equipment and technology so that these early efforts were reflections of the Russian equipment. As an example, the "August 1" produced in 1958 was a tube type machine based on the Soviet "Ural 2". Although hardware development continued, there were several factors that influenced the rate of development and although these were all political in character, they had a significant effect on the whole technological development of the nation. Computers were no exception to this hiatus. Such events as the departure of the Russians, the Great Leap and the Cultural Revolution all in their own way were instrumental in stifling a steady and continuous computer development effort. Despite these vicissitudes, lasting into the early 70s there was sporadic output. Machines such as the DJS1, DJS2, DJS7 and X2 are typical of machines of this era. These machines signified a development of second generation or transistorized machines. Some of these machines and the DJS6 which was typical of computers built in the 60s, were capable of a speed of 100 kips. The DJS6 was a 48 bit register machine with 32K internal memory. The limitation here was the memory size. Even though there is some evidence to indicate the memory available in the late 60s might have been as high as 100K, this was a serious limitation on machine capability. These machines were probably used for straightforward mathematical computations in which limited data storage or simple instructions could suffice.

Because of the demoralized state of technical and scientific personnel in the early 70s, no serious demands were made on computational capability that could not be met by the equipment generally available. The 70s however, reflected a marked increase in the amount and sophistication of computer technology. Computer designs and construction were carried out by the Chinese Academy of Sciences, the ministries having electronics responsibility and the universities. Unfortunately, the whole character of Chinese society and particularly those persons with advanced education was such that research was carried out in an individualistic manner. Progress was, therefore, of a highly provincial nature and as a result, there were a variety of computers produced, but with very little serial production . Our count shows nearly 150 different styles of machines designed and built in China by 1982, but total inventory of domestic machines probably did not exceed 3600.(12) By 1986 the number of minis and mainframes had reached 7000.(130) There had been and continues to be a generally accepted recognition of the purely technical lag and what must be done to come up to reasonably up-to-date world wide standards. For specifics, this does include the areas of computers and all their multitudinal aspects including such things as printers, modems, disk drives, memories, displays, graphics capability and software as well as components to accomplish their manufacture.

A key factor limiting mass production was and still is the low state of managerial capability in China. The Chinese leadership had come to the realization in the late 70s that this severe lack of managerial skills existed and that such skills are necessary for a sustained and efficient mass production . But the training of such persons has only recently begun and experience in this field will probably grow at a slow pace so that its impact will likely be another ten years away. This serious deficiency in managerial capability has had severe implications for serial production of computer hardware. Of the more than 150 differing varieties of computers developed in China, only about 20 have had any serial production and maybe only half that number have been produced in quantities exceeding 20 (see appendix G). The universities and the CAS still are in the single machine development stage. Although these machines, in some cases, have and will continue to become prototypes for further production, mass production is only begining to underly their developmental process. Rather, what occurs is development for a very specific need such as a research tool or data processor for a particular department or institute.

Chinese officials in the electronic sector recognized that administative interference in enterprise affairs has constrained overall efficiency and productivity. As a consequence MEI has relinquished some control over its factories.(68) Another factor limiting production is the size of the market for domestically produced machines.(130)

Specific examples of machines developed at universities that became prototypes for further production include the DJS130, developed at Qinghua University in 1974. This mini computer was designed to have similarity to Data General's Nova 1200. It has a 16 bit register, storage capacity of 64K and an operational speed of 500 kips. Although it has been used in some instances for production control, it has also enjoyed popularity at universities for research involving data processing and computations. They have been installed at South China Institute of Technology, Harbin Institute of Technology, Chengdu Institute of Telecommunications and Fudan University. The DJS130 has been programed to use BASIC, FORTRAN IV and ALGOL 60. This machine has achieved wide acceptance.(31) It represents the most widely used member of the DJS100 series which has accounted for some 700 units in operation. The success of this series of machines has encouraged the

Chinese to think in terms of further development of super minis along the line of the DJS100 series, but with several special characteristics. Hardware and software is to be compatible with the current machines; memory is to be several megabytes of MOS technology; and the use of LSI circuits for micro-minaturization is to be included.

Another machine that has had limited serial production and was designed at Fudan University is identified as the 719. At least 10 of these were eventually built by the University and located in various Shanghai universities.

Still another machine developed by Qinghua University in 1977 is the DJS050. This is a single board micro using an imported Motorola 68000 chip. It is being produced at the Anhui Radio Works (see appendix G).

Another machine, the 441B3 was designed by Tianjin University and several were built in Tianjin. It is a general purpose machine with a 24 bit register and copies are at the Municipal Commission of S&T in Tianjin and the South China Institute of Technology.

It is quite apparent from these examples that although some universities have done design and development work and have produced a working model, these machines were very infrequently used as prototypes for production models, and the number of units produced was small.

Finally, the National University of Defense Technology in a significant effort developed and produced a high speed computer called "Galaxy". The machine is reported to have a capability of 100 million ops. It was started in 1978 and was declared operational in 1983. The machine was built using imported components to expedite its construction. Two pieces of peripheral equipment built as adjuncts to the Galaxy are the Yinhe X1 a super mini being used as a preprocessor and the Yinhe F1, a simulator designed to do digital bionics.(130) There is evidence to believe that since the initial development of the Galaxy, additional Galaxys have been built and that further work by the University in either extension of the capability of the origonal machine or the development and construction of machines of greater capability has occured. A recent report indicates that difficulty with operational software has limited the usefulness of the machine. Modifications to the architecture are said to be underway to allieviate these problems. (189)

The same conclusions may be reached regarding the efforts of the CAS. Their efforts seem to be directed toward the development of special purpose high capability machines. They have been engaged in attempts to design, build and modify a high speed machine for scientific calculations. The machine is designated the 757. It was designed for scalar as well as vector processing and CAS claims a speed of up to 10 mops in the vector mode. A reporter (23) indicates that there was considerable difficulty with software development. The machine had been designed to meet the needs of the Geophysical Prospecting Bureau of the Ministry of Petroleum. Most of the design work was being done by the Institute of Computing Technology of the CAS in Beijing. Still another report (2) indicated that the then Fourth Ministry had begun work on the development of a machine to have a speed in excess of 20 mips. However, a decision was made to abandon this work since there was much duplication of the CAS work. CAS is presently under contract with the Ministry of Oil Industry to construct a modified copy of the 757 to have a speed of up to 20 mops. The machine is to be used for geologic exploration. (130) CAS has also developed a digital analog machine designated DJM330, which is a special purpose machine for solving linear equations. The Institute of Computing Technology of CAS has also been the developer of the 013 produced in 1976. It has a 48 bit word length. It is a monster. It occupies large space like US computers of the 1960s and is installed in the Computer Center CAS. This machine is presently still in use and has a speed approaching two mips. CAS seems to be devoting its efforts to special purpose machines, which will be one of a kind.

The third group operating under the Ministry of Electronics Industry (previously the 4th Ministry of Machine Building) is much more active in the development of machines for serial production. The two most important developers are the North China Institute of Computer Technology located in Beijing and the East China Research Institute of Computer Technology located some 30 kms. north of Shanghai. The North China Institute has produced an impressive array of designs including the DJS180 series (DJS183, 184, 185, and 186), the DJS200 series (DJS210, 220, 240, 260) the 109C and the 111. The DJS180 series of machines were general purpose and were built by several factories. For example, the 183 was built by the Hubei Radio Factory in four different configurations. The 184 and 186 were built by the 1915 factory, the 185 was built by the Shanghai Computer Factory. The machines were origonally designed to have speeds up to 1 mips.

The DJS200 series were computers designed in 1978. The 210 was similar to the PDP11 and the 220, 240 and 260 were patterned to be similar to the IBM 360's. The 260 had a 64 bit register and was capable of 1 to 1.5 mips. Maximum memory was 128K. These machines were also built by a variety of producers including the 1915 Factory, Peking Wire Factory, Nanjing Telecommunications Factory, Shanghai Radio Factory, Harbin Radio Factory, and Changzhou Radio Factory.

North China's latest contribution is a supermini patterned after a VAX 780 and the compatibility included both boards and software. The machine is called an NCI 2780.

The East China unit in 1965 developed the TQ16 which was a general purpose transistorized machine. It's initial design had only 25,000 ops, but the machine was gradually improved until its maximum speed was 250 kips. About 100 of these were built by the Shanghai Radio Factory under the designation 709. It had storage of up to 400k on 6 inch hard disks. Because of it's limited storage, it was limited to single task operation and was not adapted to real time operation. Two of it's uses included ship design and textile weaving design.

The 655 was developed by the East China Institute in 1973. It was an integrated circuit machine. It was in many respects similar to the 709 except that it had a speed in the range of 1 mips. These machines were built by the Shanghai Computer Factory under the designation TQ6. This was the first machine in which the magnetic disk was built in China. Twenty of the origonal design were built and other factories made copies under designations DJS11 and 150.

East China has also produced three other designs. The 1001 was a general purpose integrated circuit machine built in 1976. This machine used vertical drive magnetic disks for external storage. It was furnished with six 325 mm disks and with this extended storage was intended for real time processing.

In 1979, East China developed the HDS9. Only one machine was produced and its end use is unknown. The machine employed integrated circuits, had a 42 bit word length, had an internal storage of 512K words, and four disk drives capable of 20 mbytes each. The machine is reported to have a speed of 5 mips. Auerbach (23) gives much data on this machine.

A recent machine, the 801 developed at East China is a medium scale integrated circuit machine with imported MOS memory. The machine is an experimental machine to obtain experience with MOS technology which is still very much in the developmental stage in China. This machine was equipped with both Bulgarian and Chinese disk drives which were compatible and interchangeable. The latest machines to come out of the East China Institute are 8030 and 8060 superminis. The 8030 has compatibilty with an IBM 370/138 and the 8060 is to be a prototype and has board compatibility with an IBM 4361.

Efforts to produce micros have resulted in at least seven types that are being serially produced. The "Great Wall" is a domestic machine designed to compete with the IBM PC. The machine comes in several designations such as the 0520 the 0530A and recently the 386. The 0530A was the more powerful before the introduction of the 386 and it included a hard disk and two floppy disk drives. It has color capability, and Chinese character I/O. The machine has had reasonably good acceptance and some 2000 0520s have been exported. Other micros include the "Golden Purpose" an 8 bit machine developed by the Micro Institute of the Chengdu Institute of Radio Engineering. About 5000 are being built per year by the Nanjing #9 factory. It is patterned after the Apple II E. Another machine is called "Purple Mountain", and is built by the #734 Nanjing Telephone Exchange. Still another micro is an Apple II E copy called MCF, being produced by a private company; the Changsha Microcomputer Factory.

The Hunan Computer Factory is producing a micro called ZXJX which has an expanded keyboard including function keys to enable the machine to accept both Chinese and Western characters. About 500 of these machines have been sold. A machine called the "East Sea" was developed by the Shanghai Computer Factory. It is supposed to be a competitor to the IBM PC. Finally, the Zijin II micro was developed by an MEI unit. In order to increase sales MEI subsidized the purchase of Great Walls and Zijin IIs in the amount of one million Yuan for electronic institutes and engineering colleges under its umbrella.(134) Sales

16

difficulties produced other suggestions. In a column by Mao Zhihui, economic problems were identified as impacting the marketing of computers. The writer suggested a practise of purchasing computers under an installment plan through a program of rental and loan service through banks.(156) This approach would not solve the problem that most Chinese families face in that they cannot afford to buy personal computers when prices range from $2500 for an Apple II to $30,000 for an IBM PC when the annual income of a Chinese worker is less than 1000 Yuan RMB.(163)

It appears that a tacit division of responsibility for computer development exists; that research mostly occurs at the universities and the Academy; design for special purpose at the Academy; and that most prototype development is carried out by the institutes of the Ministry of Electronics Industry. While they are all active in all areas their primary objectives are as indicated. A furthur division is that MEI has responsibility for micros and minis, CAS has responsbility for general purpose machines having speeds between 10 and 100 mops, and the National University of Defense Technology is responsible for large machines having speeds of 100 mops or more.(130)

There is much effort in China at this time directed toward the development of systems for character recognition. In effect, the Chinese ~~product~~ are looking for a Chinese character word processor and/or data processor. The machine would almost fit the requirements of an intelligent terminal. It would certainly have to be China user friendly. Work was in progress at nearly every university we visited regarding this subject. The Academy was also undertaking some effort in this area, as was the Ministry of Electronics Industry. The Chinese are very excited regarding the desireability of such computing equipment that can accept and display Chinese characters. A report in the China Daily says "priority should be given to the development of...Chinese character terminal systems." (122)

Another statement in China Computerworld points out that for Chinese character word processing the use of an intelligent terminal has compatibility with a variety of computers. (54) At a trade show in September 1982 displaying Chinese word processors, more than 30 different models were being demonstrated. Most of the machines were assembled in China, a few were of Japanese origin and none were from the US or any other country. However, an examination of the literature on the Chinese machines showed that all of them were using US made microprocessors. Another national exhibition of word processors was conducted in Beijing in April 1988. In 1988 the China Information Processing Research Center affiliated with the Beijing Information Technology Institute developed a Chinese character recognition system and speaker-independent voice recognition system. Recognition speed on a microcomputer is said to be eight characters per second. Ultimately only a few of the many systems under development will survive.

One of the stated objectives in China is to popularize the usage of computers. To this end, the East China Institute was working toward the development of software for their latest mini-computers for industrial control, railroad management, tourism and air reservation. Future objectives for this unit as expressed by them are the development of prototype minis and micros for popular use in industry; the development of software packages to popularize the use of computers and the development of such peripheral equipment as printers, plotters, terminals, memory devices, and displays.

Recent developments in China include SJ55/40 mid-range minis, the 056B and C, eight bit micros, the use of a USS063 for control of metal working machinery and the DJS130 used for data base management. Also reported was the CCS-1 micro developed by the Hunan Electronic Technology Research Institute and Changsha Railway Engineering Institute for a file management system . (26) This system can recieve both Chinese characters and ASCII codes.

Other developments include the production of 13 new types of CMOS products which meet the new Chinese national standards which conform to the current international standards. Recently developed is an HZ-82 intelligent terminal which displays Chinese characters. The terminal performs parallel processing.(13)

Software, Peripherals and Computer Components

Software development has followed hardware development. It is in a one-of-a-kind state, since each hardware developer has had to produce his own software and little serial production has occurred. With the importation of much computing equipment, there is increased production of software adaptable to a large variety of this imported equipment. According to one report, "China's apparent goal is to develop its own software industry and sell software products to domestic and international markets. The strategy has two stages, develop a production base for stand alone applications packages and expand the base to create a production capability for systems and real time control software".(169)

Organizations devoted to software production for all varieties of machines and all varieties of users are springing up all over the nation. In January 1984 the China Software Technique Corp. became an autonomous enterprise under MEI with a network of 19 branches in provinces and municipalities and with 20 more branches planned. The Corporation has two functions, managing software businesses and serving as a center of software technology development. Support may be from private contracts, provincial or municipal governments, ministries, CAS, or the central government. The corporation has recently undertaken to produce a law to protect software producers from copiers. Such a law does not exist in China in 1988 and with the proliferation of software producers copying is on the increase.

Another organization called Beijing Stone Group was formed in 1984 as a private venture primarily devoted to developing both software and hardware for the Chinese character word processing demand. The group has become the major player in the Chinese electronics industry with a

Chinese-English word processing typewriter printer its major product.

Universities have also been developing application software packages. Beijing University, Nanjing University, Qinghua University, Jiaotong (Shanghai) University, Jilin University, are all involved. Typical packages include laser photocomposition for Chinese characters, DBMS, product testing, graphics, financial analysis, expert systems and artificial intelligence.

Peripheral development lags behind computer and software development. Primary emphasis has been on the development of hardware, and although some peripherals are to be seen, they are few, far between and none too reliable.

Component development has meant emphasis on integrated circuits. But such simple components as metal film resistors that meet required industry standards cannot be produced in China even though more than 10 factories are in production on this item. The Chinese claim to have mastered the technology to make ICs consisting of up to ten thousand elements and to produce them in batches by 1986. Designs for ICs having elements in excess of ten thousand have been finalized and many of the key materials such as super pure gases and super pure reagents are meeting production needs.(127) In 1985 reports vary regarding chip yield ranging from 20% for complicated structures to 95% for simple structures.(130) However, the external chip universe is constantly widening the gap with work being done on the megachip and the superchip for central processing units. As a result in 1988 many of these items are still imported.


## MODERNIZING AND UPGRADING


### Roles of Foreign Computers

Over the years, the Chinese have imported equipment from many countries. We have been able to find reports on imports from USA, Japan, Russia, Australia, England, Canada, France, Germany, Hungary, Italy, Poland, Norway, Romania, and Sweden. By far the greatest exporters have been the US with Japan following close behind. The remaining countries have had few exports in comparison. Examination of the details of imported computing equipment tends to indicate that the Chinese have a healthy appetite for all sorts of computing equipment for all sorts of applications. There is one area, however, that especially stands out in their purchases. The area of data processing for geophysical exploration which translates into petroleum source discovery is strongly supported by imported equipment. There are 25 known installations engaged in this kind of endeavor. They include Control Data Corporation 720s, 730s, 750s, and an IBM 3033 which, although located in China and operated by Chinese personnel, is owned by Western Geophysical of Texas who is responsible for its operation. Digital Equipment has PDP 11/45s and

Perkin Elmer some 3220s all being used for oil and gas prospecting. Sperry Univac has several 1100 machines, Hitachi has several M160s, Sintrex of Canada has a unit, and the French have an IRIS 50 all devoted to petroleum exploration data processing. Except for a Hitachi M180 approved by COCOM for rail traffic control, some of these machines were until recently the most powerful machines in non military uses in China. In 1986, however with the relaxation of COCOM restrictions a CDC Cyber 180-845 and a 180-855 were delivered for use in the Zhongyuan and Daqing oil fields.(147) Their combination of large data storage and fast operating speed make them of great importance in data processing of large quantities of data. The second area of some interest as evidenced by purchases of foreign computing equipment is data or information management. Burroughs has a B3950 a B6810, and in 1985 a computer network system with a mainframe capable of 2.5 mops in operation at Huafeng Computer Center. Hewlitt Packard has several 3000 Series III machines, IBM has a 3032 in Hong Kong at the Bank of China, and there is a Prime 550 at the China Tourist Bureau. Fujitsu has a FACOM M160 at Tianjin in the Municipal Computer Center. The Beijing Municipal Computer Center has a Burroughs 6800 and a Wang VS 80. The Liaoning Provincial Computer Center has a Roumanian Felix 512, and the Hunan Provincial Computer Center has a Hitachi M150. Also, Hitachi has a M180 used for rail traffic control, Mitsubishi is installing a system for reservations at a Guangzhou hotel and Nippon Electric has a 300 being used for inventory control in Shanghai. In addition to these installations, the IBM machines provided by the UN for the census will be used in part as information retrieval centers although it is expected the data will be used to provide an understanding of the demographics of China's population situation. Other areas being served by imported computers are seismology, travel service activities, air traffic control, management of container port facilities, meteorology, and hydrologic studies. Industrial installations include the Shenyang Boiler Works which uses an IBM 370/138 for factory process control, a large polyester plant using Honeywell process control, and the Baoshan Steel Plant using 16 Hitachi mini processors.

The third area that has become of recent interest to the Chinese is the training of personnel that can take advantage of the opportunities provided by a sophisticated computer facility. Evidence of this situation can best be seen at the universities. By far the most important event to have taken place in this regard was the recent determination to provide up-to-date computational equipment by purchases through a loan from the World Bank. This equipment has been placed at leading universities around the country. As a subsequent phase the World Bank is financing loans for ministry acquisition of computers. (130) In our discussion with universities it was stressed that these installations would be used in the dual capacity as a teaching tool to develop student expertise and as a research tool available for faculty and researchers on the university campus.

The first group of the World Bank machines included US made

Honeywell mid size DPS-8 systems and Japanese AI micros. In addition orders were placed in 1985 for the Bull Co. (France) to send DPS-7 main frames, DPS-6 minis, Questar terminals and 30 Micral micros to China.(154) Acquisition of machines through the World Bank loan represents the latest effort on the part of the universities and the Ministry of Education to upscale training and computer knowledge. Reports indicate Honeywell has seventeen mainframes and 100 DPS-6 minis installed in China.(141) Recent imported significant acquisitions by universities include a DEC VT100, an IBM 5550 and a Honeywell DPS 852 at Jiaotung, Xian, and Honeywell DPS6 minis at several universities including the People's University in Beijing, and the University of South China. Other acquisitions include DEC PDP machines at Qinghua University, Beijing University, Tianjin University, Fudan University, and Northwest Telecommunications Engineering Institute in Xian. Jiaotung, Xian has also acquired a Prime 550 and a Prime 640 is installed at the Beijing Institute of Aeronautics and Astronautics. Sperry has a 1100 machine at the Beijng University of Science and Technology and there is a Wang machine at Jiaotung, Shanghai. Fujitsu has recently been sucessful in placing a FACOM M140 at the University of Science and Technology at Hefei and an M150 at Qinghua. Both of these installations are very well done. They have been installed in newly renovated air conditioned, well lighted, clean quarters. The installations look like what one might see in a US university. The machines are equipped with multiple terminals, printers and plotters. Tianjin University also had a Honeywell DPS8 and a DPS6. Sichuan University was reported to have a Hitachi M 240 and a M 340. The University of Science and Technology in Hefei also has a Honeywell DPS 8, a Gould 32/2750 and a VAX 11/750. The National University of Defense Technology has a Honeywell DPS 6. In addition, there are Roumanian Felix C256 machines at Northwest Polytechnic University at Xian and at the Beijing Institute of Aeronautics and Astronautics. Northwest also has a VAX 11/780, and a Prime 552. At Northeast Polytechnic University in Shenyang a NEC ACOS 400 is installed. The Chengdu Institute of Radio Engineering has a VAX 11/780 and four PDP 11/24s. At all of the universities, US micros were much in evidence, many of them being located in personal laboratories of professors at the various campuses as well as specialty labs of the Institutes of the Academy. Most commonly seen before 1980 were Cromemco machines, although Radio Shack TRS80's were also in evidence. By 1985 many IBM PC's were to be seen throughout China. Examples of gifts of foreign computers are a Hewlitt-Packard 3000 series 68 mini with peripherals to the Department of Computer Science and Technology of Beijing University, and 100 IBM 5550 multi purpose micros for Beijing, Qinghua, Fudan and Jiaotung Shanghai Universities.

Other micros included Commodore, Apple, Alpha, Computervision, Hewlitt Packard, and Hughes. It is interesting to note that microcomputing in China is essentially all done on US micros. There appears to be few Japanese or domestic machines available in China, although there is evidence of a growing supply of Chinese assembled micros, particularly Great Wall machines.

Some imported computers and their sources are listed in appendix H.

## Impact of Foreign Specialists and Knowledge

The Chinese in an effort to improve the timeliness of their technology, have made strenuous efforts to bring specialists into the country to discuss the state of knowledge in the world at large and computers in particular. Grey in his book on Aeronautics in China (30), Garner in his report on Computing in China (31), Auerbach in his IEEE report (23) and Sherman in his report on Electrotechnology in China (24) have all indicated inputs made to the Chinese on the state of their computational facilities and compared them to that of more advanced nations. Although we have little direct evidence of the availability of current literature in the computer field in China, there seemed to be a substantial understanding by those computer professionals contacted regarding the state of the art.

A factor in the acquisition of knowledge regarding computers outside of China has been the large number of Chinese technical and scientific persons who have traveled and studied in advanced technological countries. Of those 30 or so students and visiting professionals from China with which the authors have had direct contact, all have availed themselves of the opportunity to obtain hands on experience with US computers and many have spent much time in discussion with science and engineering persons involved in new directions in the field. In the few instances where these Chinese persons have been able to obtain industrial experience in the US, their activities invariably involve the use of computational facilities.

The Chinese, therefore, are well aware of the necessity for the development of a knowledgable cadre of trained computer persons. Further evidence is to be had by observing their invitations to specialists to visit China as well as allowing visits of their own specialists abroad. The effort is to expose their own specialists to the influence of foreign innovation.

## Summary

Bus.
Env.

Leadership in China is very aware of the importance of computational capability if the country is ever to raise its technical competence anywhere near that of the more advanced countries in the world. The Chinese don't lack in basic knowledge of computers or computational ability. To develop a technological base, however, will require an extensive effort in time, money and activity. The modernization of their computer capability will depend on how well they can train competent personnel, develop an industrial base to furnish necessary components, develop software, manufacture peripheral equipment and finally construct the actual computing machines. While all this is happening, it must be done in consort with the latest technological developments taking place in other countries. A formidable task, to say the least.

Although much effort is now being expended in training a coterie of computer specialists, there is still only a limited number of students studying in areas related to computers. This will change rapidly because of the effort on popularization. In fact, with the rapid increase of mini and micro computer availability on campuses, training efforts can quickly become the area which will show the fastest improvement. The big bulge in numbers will not occur for the next five years. Training will probably not be a negative factor for long in computer development and usage.

Modern development of the computer will probably continue to be a factor in development of widespread use of computers. The present day scene calls for minis and micros, but China still has not been able to produce hard disk memory devices and must still rely on tape memory devices or imported hard disk drives for their machines. For micros the Chinese still do not have single chip microprocessors with more than eight bit capacity while both the US and Japan are busily producing machines with 16 and 32 bit registers. China's ability to produce 16 bit microprocessors is still at least five years away even if they copy presently available technology.

CMOS technology is the presently preferred storage semiconductor. Mass production of this technology does not exist in China. Again, this technology is at least five years away. Even if China does develop this and other similar technologies in five years, other countries will have moved into new territories. The Chinese show little indication of trying to move beyond their present technologies now. In 1984 Dorado Co. of the US sold a microchip programmer to Shanghai Instrument and Electronics Bureau that should help in this regard.(186) In the meantime, the US and Japanese are pursuing with excitement and fervor such ideas as non Von Neuman machines, massive parallelism, data flow, MOS VSLI chips, VHSIC, chip splicing, high fault tolerance, and highly friendly speech recognition devices.These ideas are still only in the talking stage in China. While China continues to expect to send technical types abroad our experience is that these persons can't wait to work with US computers. The time lag in getting state-of-the-art information into the streams of computer design will still be years away.

Considerable activity is taking place in CAD work of all sorts but the machines being used are all imports. An example can be found in the recent order to CALMA Co. a subsidiary of General Electric USA for 60 CAD/CAED Apollo computer based work stations with Calma Dimension 3 architecture-engineering-construction software. (148) There is a smattering of development work in some of the basic areas as well as work in some forefront areas. There is work presently underway in such areas as pattern recognition, robotics, forms of artificial intelligence and Chinese character recognition, but with the exception of Chinese character recognition, these efforts are small with few people engaged in their activities.

The most difficult problem the Chinese face is the mass production of computational equipment. Included must be hardware of all sorts such as main frames or central processing units, and peripherals such as disk drives, printers, plotters and terminals. Even though their best designs such as the HDS 801 are not up to US or Japanese standards for quality and computational capability, they still are quite adequate for a large number of such applications as data management, data processing, and control operations. But such machines are not produced in large quantities. As already indicated, one factor involved is the lack of breadth and depth of the Chinese market for domestic machines as a result of the demand for foreign equipment. Although China is aware of the limited domestic production of machines and peripherals, it will take at least five years for them to mount production facilities adequate to produce such hardware at a rate ten times their present rate.

There is also the question of software development. A dual problem exists in this regard. With the large number of imports China is using, they should be developing a software capability that is compatible with these machines. Instead, they seem to be continuing to rely primarily on the software packages available from the manufacturers of the basic domestic machines. Software development by comparison in the US is taking place at a great rate by a burgeoning number of small outfits that are producing a great variety of compatible programs.

Software development in China for minis and mid size machines has in the past been done by municipal and provincial centers. The slow pace of software development has been due to the lack of understanding of the importance of a marketing effort. The new emphasis on entrepreneurship and the consequent emergence of small and medium size organizations willing to provide software service for profit should bring about a surge of software for these machines.

The end result of the slow development of software will most likely extend the dependence of the Chinese on imported computers and software. Further it appears that the great advantage the US now enjoys in the variety of software packages available will enhance its competitive position for the sale of all aspects of computer technology to China. In fact, several technical persons in China have voiced their decided preference for US computer equipment and mentioned the great variety of software as one factor in their decision.

Then there are peripherals. As with the software situation, very little in the way of plotters, terminals, storage devices, or printers have been produced in China. This is also an area in which their lag is great. They will continue to be behind the rest of the world for a long time to come. There appears to be only a small effort toward development of these auxiliaries and only at the two computer institutes of the Ministry of Electronics Industry.

## TRENDS AND IMPLICATIONS

### Trends

At the compeletion of the 1978-85 plan, and Fang Yi's Ten (plus) Commandments for the China computer world, certain trends are clearly discernible. The significant trends are:

* Chinese announcements of achievement tend to lead the facts
* Rapid growth of a comprehensive and almost burdensome computer structure with some elite characteristics
* Expanded application supported by strong popularization efforts
* Domestic sales problems lead to price subsidization of Great Wall and Zijin II micros by MEI
* Lack of coordination of geographical location of developers and manufacturers
* Continuation of weak factory management
* Geographic dispersion of centers and production capacity
* Greater emphasis on ICs and in particular, VLSICs and plans for Wuxi
* Recognition of the importance of the actual start of serialized mass production but production of fewer models with emphasis on minis and micros
* An awakening to production incentives and the value of market analysis
* More emphasis on maintenance and service
* Initial moves on and additional planning for networks and network development
* More emphasis on software
* Strong continued support of basic research in the universities through the US NSF counterpart
* Greater emphasis on a variety of approaches for producing a growing spectrum of technically trained manpower
* Outreach for help through UN, World Bank, and US NSF protocols
* Educational, military and scientific and technological reforms of 1985 which focuses on applied research and development activities
* An emphasis on acquistion of technology and training support through joint ventures
* Competitive infiltration of the Chinese computer market
* Potential protectionism
* Emphasis on entrepreneurship in universities and research institutes of both the CAS and MEI, which includes consulting by professional employees of these organizations
* Decentralization of MEI factory control

Implications

The achievement of uniform substantial progress does not exist. Progress is in fact spotty and the implications of a whole series of problems will continue to influence progress for some time to come.These problems and their implications are as follows.

Applications. In 1984 approximately 72,000 micros were imported while 27,000 were produced domestically. The result was a computer market glut that left 40,000 micros unused. As a conequence MEI decided to set aside one million Yuan to subsidize domestic computer purchases. The intent was to reduce inventory and popularize the use of the Great Wall and the Zijin II. (134) Another source reports that in 1985 less than half of the 130,000 micros were being used. The computer industry had an inventory of 20,000 unsold domestic computers at the end of 1985. (142) Also in 1985 MEI carried out a national computer commodity fair to promote the use of computer technology in the transformation of traditional enterprises and to speed up computer application in all sectors of the economy.(157)

In the years 1983-86 universities and research institutes were encouraged to develop products for sale on a contract basis. They were also encouraged to become involved in installation, maintenance and service. The most interesting part of the contract approach involved a payback from the end user to the developer related to the profit impact of the installed equipment. The incentive was real since it was emphasized by a reduction in funds from the central government.

Technical Problems. These problems are related to

* Memory and storage capacity and the constraints that follow
* Serial production involving precision machining and
    manufacturing paricularly for high technical items
* Implementation of national computer standards and rapid
    improvement in this area
* Sophisticated technology indigestion

Manpower Problems. These problems involve

* Inability of output to cope with demand
* The aged obsolete training of the senior computer cadre
* General isolation of the computer manpower pool from the
    cutting edge of equipment and knowledge
* Seeming absence of sound, carefully developed policy for
    allocation of quality personnel between military, education,
    research and factory efforts. The educational reforms of 1985
    may bring some improvement in the situation. Further
    improvement may result from the February 1987 State Council
    reform of the S & T system. The reform will hasten the

integration of scientific research and industrial production. 5000 research institutes and 7000 large and medium size enterprises will be merged by 1990.

* Continuing uncertain status of the intellectual including computer experts given such problems as mounting pressure to produce and reaction to job displacement or the ills of featherbedding.
* Need for improved technically trained management capable of coping with the problems of sophistication and precision production

Special Barriers. These barriers are

* COCOM regulations.
* Absence of precision machinery in China and inability to develop it.
* The isolation created by vertical integration.
* Inadequate electric power production capability.
* Inadequate telecommunication capability.
* Inadequate development of multidisciplinary approaches.

Power Struggles and Policy Split. There appears to be either the possibility of change or a confrontation in the different language of Wang Xinggang of the CAS Institute of Technology, emphasizing market forecasting that pinpoints economic and social budgets as opposed to a more narrow approach designed to meet military needs. However, Jiang Zemin, former Minister of Electronics says "the Ministry will give priority to the development of electronic goods used by the military and let the production of these goods stimulate the civilian production." (129) Also there appears to be the potential of conflict or change between the role of the State Science and Technology Commission in establishing a bureau with responsibility for collection, processing and distributing scientific and technical information which had been previously described as the function of the Yan Shan Science and Technology Corporation of the CASS, which some people reported had military ties or missions.

According to Simon and Rehn (68), Chinese leaders wish to establish several electronics research production centers modeled on Silicon Valley. These centers would concentrate on several strategic fields such as LSICs, new materials and micros. Beijing has been selected as one site for a center, however the selection of a second site involves a struggle between the municipal government of Shanghai and MEI. The State Council's Leading Group for the Invigoration of the Electronics Industry consistent with its harmonizing role will attempt the resolution of disputes of this nature. Preliminary discussions in January 1986 indicated the possibility of a compromise which will allow Shanghai to concentrate on the production of memory chips for computers and industrial applications while MEI will have Wuxi focus on ICs for consumer electronics.

Another area of struggle contributing to unevenness is found in the apparently unresolved question of the balance between domestic production and foreign imports. According to Sigurdson, (32) the future of China's computer industry is far from clear and the debate centers on two major approaches. One group advocates that China should adopt the world's most popular models and copy them in domestic plants. Thus, software would be easily available in China. A second approach advocates that China must carry out its own independent development. Major reasons for this are that it would allow China much more freedom in the choice of technology and in the choice of components. The issue is further complicated by the demand from the users for more computers and particularly imports and complaints from the domestic manufacturers who do not want to get shunted away.(163)

In 1986 Vice Premier Li Peng told the country's electronic industry that their most important task was to utilize domestic components in the manufacture of products even though China would continue to import advanced technology.(145) To realize this goal China must resolve the many problems afflicting its domestic computer industry among which are the improvement of precision manufacture and the reduction in the cost of production.

Market Competition. In 1984-85 relaxation of COCOM regulations helped accelerate the Chinese acquisition of foreign equipment. As a result foreign currency reserves were rapidly depleted. China then increased import duties and pushed for the inclusion of technology transfer and training assistance as an integral part of sales contracts. As a result, China had added to the leverage of preference for foreign equipment by providing the opportunity for the manufacturing, sales, service and training infrastructures to expand.

Comparison with the external world. China had fourth generation computers based on LSICs by 1983. They reported in 1984 the achievement of the 10 million ops CAS vector computer and the 100 million ops computer which was developed at the National University of Defense Technology. CAS is presently engaged in producing a machine with an expected speed of 20 mops. The leading countries of the computer world have fourth generation computers based on VHSICs and they are talking about fifth generation machines. Others also can do over 100 million ops and are discussing 10 bflops. For example the CRAY II became available in the US in 1985.

Another interesting comparison is how China ranked in number of computers per million of non-agriculture labor force. Table 1.1 shows the Chinese having an approximate 200% increase in number of computers per million of non-agricultural labor force population between 1976 and 1982. The 1976 figures, reflect that China was substantially behind the US and Japan but that it might be opening a gap between itself and India. Contrasted to this data though, are 1983 reports reflecting a projected growth rate for the Chinese computer industry ranging from 20 - 40% annually, although 40% is doubted by the engineers at the Ministry of Electronics Industry.

TABLE 1.1
Computers Per Non-agricultural Labor Force.

| Country | Estimated computer installations 1976 | | Non-agricul. labor force (in millions) 1976 | 1982 | Number of computers per million non-ag labor force 1976 | 1982 |
|---------|------|------|------|------|------|------|
| | 1976 | 1982 | 1976 | 1982 | 1976 | 1982 |
| China | 1000 | 4000 | 60 | 80 | 17 | 50 |
| USA | 170,000 | ---- | 92 | 1847 | 1850 | |
| Japan | 39,000 | ---- | 47 | 829 | 10000 | |
| India | 350 | | 60 | 6 | 6 | |

However, inventory and production shown in Table 1.2 tend to indicate a confused picture suggesting little reliability in growth projections.

Summary

The implications of having a rapidly expanding computer structure, isolated from the cutting edge of equipment and machining, in short supply of technically trained manpower and headed for a confrontation with the issue of job displacement with inadequate offset capability are enormous.

The rapid expansion is placing the capability to produce technically trained manpower under stress. It is stressing the selection and placement process. It will ultimately put academia at a variety of levels under great pressure. Academia will be simultaneously pressed on the manpower front and on the R&D front. Pressure will come on the R&D front because of

TABLE 1.2
China Computer Inventory and Production

| | Inventory Large, medium & small | micros | Production in 1982 Large, medium & small | micros |
|---|---|---|---|---|
| 1980 | 2600 | unknown | 241 | 7028 |
| 1981 | 3945 | 10,000 | | |
| 1982(33) | 4000 | 10,000+ | | |
| 1986(130) | 7000 | 130,000 | | |

the strengthening of the basic R&D funding and the encouragement of entrepreneurial activities in Chinese colleges and universities and the partial isolation induced by COCOM regulations. Technical problems relating to memory expansion and precision manufacture stand in the way of data base development, expanded storage, large scale data processing efforts, and real time work. They stand in the way of rapid military command control response, working with massive data bases, and they stand in the way of sophisticated simultaneous calculation and more and more reliability.

Isolated by the ambivalence of a schizophrenic US policy which alternately treats China as a quasi ally and then as a communist country, China can't produce what it needs to achieve breakthroughs on VLSICs, VHSICs, large computers except on a one-of-a-kind basis with the 10 million and 100 million ops computers. Unless the visits of the US Secretary of Defense, the Defense Minister of China, the Premier of China, and the President of the US and others bring change, they will continue to be pushed toward self reliance at certain levels. The consequence is that their efforts to obtain the necessary machines, equipment, and technology will become more and more strident out of frustration and will involve bogus companies and may involve industrial espionage. It was reported in 1984 that production equipment for CMOS and TTL chips had been sold to Hua-Ko a Hong Kong fabricator owned by China. According to the report if this semiconductor capability is available to the Chinese there is very little that they can't make.(185) Recognizing these pressures, COCOM regulations were relaxed and modified by 1985 to broaden the "green zones" of controls. Included in the relaxed controls are certain computer systems, I/O control units, array processors, and silicon based microprocessors.(138,139)

The China Daily in January 1984, reported Fang Yi, Minister in charge of State Science and Technology Commission, as announcing an effort to establish a nationwide computer based S&T service which would provide access to foreign S&T information. Assisting this development was the satellite linking of a few Chinese institutes to American and European information systems. In April of 1984, an Associated Press report indicated that China put into orbit an experimental communication satellite. This is a significant step forward, especially if the satellite is geosynchronous allowing continuous computer contact with the satellite. The satellite is reported, however, to be unstable in its orbit making continous contact unreliable. The Chinese with the help of the Canadians have a new stable geosynchronous satellite in orbit in 1988.

The Chinese are expending much time in the development of Chinese character representation. One reads and hears of highly trained professionals at many institutions and universities actively trying to work on this problem. The need for more and varied computer capability to popularize usage may be hampered by the time spent on character representation development. However, it is hard to assess how meaningful any of the more than ten Chinese systems under study may be. Perhaps there is a chance that the Chinese will come in first in the race to develop a Chinese character processing system.

China's only hope for significant improvement on a very large scale by the year 2000 is through acquisition of foreign systems, co-production joint ventures, technology acquisition and transfer and abatement of potentially high level stresses in the system. Perhaps this is characteristic of an exploratory transition period. Supportive of this point of view is the fact that the general manager of China's Import and Export Corp. announced that China's import program in the short term will concentrate on acquiring technological innovations in the microcomputer industry and technology for mass production of high efficiency high quality electronic components. (140). A slow down of all imported computer products will probably occur because of an increase in import tax levels instituted in January 1985. Retarding rapid improvment is the fact that IBM appears to be cutting back their China operation because of 1985 import restrictions that reduced the number of micros imported. However, the motivation of IBM in this matter is obscure. It may be that IBM's cuback is intended to improve the accommodation of the Chinese.(144) Earlier in the latter part of 1985 IBM was more positive about its relationship to China and its sales volume.(151)

## PROBLEMS AND DEFICIENCIES

### Priority and Resource Allocation

Resource allocation raises several questions. Have the Chinese thought through, carefully enough, the major joint venture investment effort? Because of problems and deficiencies, is the only hope foreign equipment acquisition? Is technology acquisition supported by vastly improved precision production the answer? Must the Chinese in the final analysis, beyond the year 2000, depend on themselves?

Our analysis is that although computers do not have the highest priority in resource allocation, the resources that are available are evenhandedly divided between the various organizations responsible for the development of computational capability.

### Manpower

What of the likelihood of increasing the supply of technically trained manpower and the allocation of a quality cut to the factory world? Chinese universities had just started to turn out post Cultural Revolution graduates in 1982 and 1983. This output should tend to increase with the percentage input of middle school graduates entering universities rising from 5% to 13%.(70) With the corresponding growth in the number of computer departments, computer faculty, laboratories and equipment, the supply problem will become less acute. By 1986 there were already indications that the situation was improving. In 1987 cooperative ties were established between fourteen plants under MEI and Qinghua University. The plants purchased $460,000 worth of equipment for an electrical circuits laboratory. In exchange the university will provide training to the factory scientists and technicians supplying them with technological advancements in integrated circuits. Further help in alleviating the problem will come from the activities and programs of still other institutions of higher learning being complemented by lower level training efforts. There has been a call for lower level training in intermediate vocational schools as early as 1980. The fact was stressed that China in 1980 could train 2000 people a year in the computer area, or 20,000 in a decade. The magnitude of the problem was stressed by pointing out that China needed 100,000 personnel to operate and maintain its computers in 1980 and that it would need 500,000 in 1990 (this latter figure is probably high).(29) If 500,000 is a realistic need figure, it is very doubtful that the education-training systems as modified by the 1985 reforms can cope with such a demand. Evidence of this is the Epsom attempt to sue the Industrial Development Service Co. of Shenzen over their inability to procure satisfactorily skilled workers.(143) The above numbers do not include software engineering manpower requirements. In 1985 it was estimated that 10,000 persons were working in the software development area and that the requirements for this arena alone would be 100,000 by 1995.(160)

### Planning and Management

Before production there must be planning of what is to be accomplished and prioritizing to cope with problem technology areas. In the past China has placed too much emphasis on prototype development, one of a kind activity, and a preoccupation with hardware as opposed to peripherals and software. This is gradually changing with attempts at serialization, mass production, and joint ventures aimed at acquiring peripheral and software expertise and technology. These latter efforts include training as well as technology acquisition. While the Chinese recognize the importance of peripherals and software, they are weak in these areas and are just starting to address them. They have also identified several other critical priority areas such as semiconductor chip technology, the production of hard disk devices, and the VLSIC area. So far, achievments have been limited. While the question might have been asked in the past; have the Chinese really recognized or know what they need? They are now giving evidence that they do know.

Severe lack of managerial skills have in the past had some responsibility for slow computer development but recently there has been much effort in improving these skills resulting in decentralization of management responsibility with a consequent improvement in all areas related to computers.

## Design

Before commenting on production, it is necessary to point out that civilian and military design criteria are not always complementary from the point of view of a clash between priority and popularization. The reason for stressing this point is the size of the military budget, and the consequent impact of defense priorities on computer design because a very significant percentage of Chinese computers are used in the military and industry related to the military.

## Machining Production and Standards

Precision machining capability limits production capability in the computer business. The ability to manufacture parts under very high precision is a serious limitation in China. Following design comes the production process itself. In some areas production appears to be constrained by the size and depth of the domestic market because of the impact of imports. A memory device expert has expressed a concern that the present technical force in factories appears to be weaker than the work force in scientific research organizations and institutions of higher learning. (28) Quality of manpower impacts quality control. Standards impact quality control and work in the standards area is progressing but continues to need attention. Progress is evidenced by a national meeting in Guangzhou that approved detailed rules and regulations on total quality control in the computer industry, tentative regulations on awards for quality production in the computer industry, detailed rules and regulations concerning a license system for computer products and detailed rules and regulations on quality control in war production.(173) Also inadequate supply of technically trained manpower impacts distribution of manpower and quality control. All of these things coalesce in many areas of Chinese manufacture. An outstanding example is their impact on precision parts production which has been their chief difficulty in the production of disk drives and integrated circuits.

## Motivation and Incentives

A more subtle question arises that relates to behavior of computer personnel. Has the 12th Congress adequately reassured intellectuals, scientists, engineers, and technicians of stability in their future? The student demonstrations in late 1986 and early 87 emhasize the continuing relevance of this question. The question has certainly raised the doubts of the intellectuals and university faculty and researchers. China has recently again taken special pains to assure the intellectuals, particularly those engaged in scientific and technological pursuits that they must continue to be bold in dealing with academic problems and be ready to express different views. However, a distinction is being made. Qian Xuesen, chairman of CAST said,"We must never label rashly the different views and understanding over academic problems of natural science as advocating bourgeois liberalization."(188)

Is China as a consequence of these perturbations in a position to optimize its computer achievments? This may depend upon how the central government develops policies that impact creative ideas and initiatives of this group of people. As the onrush of the 21st century computer world takes over and there is a rising fear of automation, will the computer expert be vilified and expended, protected and put on a leash or discarded? Management has not been sufficiently agressive in handling the problem of surplus of non-technically trained personnel.

It seems that these uncertainties and the fear induced by them will tend to stand in the way of bold initiatives, dramatic achievments and breakthroughs.

## Network Constraints

Once the equipment is in place and operating, problems of time sharing, conciousness of need for more data base creation, data storage and retrieval and the benefit of networking to optimize the use of the investment all impinge. Time sharing is not widespread and data bases are just developing and are few and far between. However, UN involvement is pushing this effort forward. Networking is now generally outside of Chinese capability because of deficiencies in their existing communication system ranging from quality of lines to age of switch gear. Work that is going on as late as 1986 is largely experimental and very limited. Most of the network research work is going on in research institutes or at universities. However, by 1988 China possesses a stable geosynchronous satellite which will enhance the networking ability and accelerate the rate of progress in this area .(130)

## Isolation of Vertical Integration

Based on field experience of September 1982, it would appear that while the Chinese Academy of Sciences and the Ministry of Electronics Industry both have elements intimately involved in the computer world, there has been much reluctance to foster interaction. In early 1987 the State Council has attempted to hasten activities leading to extensive scientific and technological cooperation between research institutes and industry.

To the degree that vertical integration continues to persist, and isolation of groups or substructures occur, this will get in the way of optimizing the use of resources and ultimately retard achievement. It would appear that these limits to interaction will continue to get in the way of both initiative and the acceleration of achievement for some time to come.

## Utilization

It is necessary to look at effort and investment to see what is at stake in underutilization. By the end of 1983, China expected to have between 4500 and 5000 large, medium and small computers plus 11,000 or more micros. China spent substantially over 1000 million Yuan in importing between 550-600 standard computers and well over 10,000 micros.(33) The 1985 production goal was 1000 standard computers and 10,000 micros and single boards. It would appear that this optimistic goal was not being achieved. However, domestic production and volume of imports indicate both a substantial effort and investment. A sizeable inventory is in the making. Once the computer arrives from abroad, what happens? Delivered equipment sits in warehouses for periods of time and even after arriving at the user site, many times it takes a lengthy time period to get the equipment operating. Corruption, manpower, and expertise are involved in underutilization of what is becoming more and more of a major asset. A 1982 report indicated that less than 1/3 of the computers in China operated more than 10 hours a day. It went on to indicate that only three out of 234 computers in Anhui Province operated over eight hours a day.(3) A 1980 report indicated conditions had been worse:

* 1/3 of the computers were idle
* 1/3 of the computers were not used properly
* 1/3 of the computers were used properly (29)

The problem continues in the form of 14,000 micros being used less than three hours a day.(135)  Erratic performance of power supplies and disk drives are a complicating factor. In addition, electricity is subject to cut off due to lack of sufficient generating capacity. While the Chinese are properly annoyed about delay related to US and COCOM approvals, and are putting penalty clauses in equipment contracts to pressure U.S. companies, there are other problems. Dramatic improvement is needed. The growing service structure undoubtedly will help.

## Explosiveness of the Computer World

While China is getting a respectable structure together and trying to build a manpower base, the rest of the computer world is making dramatic achievements with micros and planning parallel processing and 10 to 100 billion floating point operating performance. This explosiveness makes it difficult for the Chinese to compete in the market place. Complicating matters is the fact that China is acquiring technology today, entering into major and in some cases long term relationships to capitalize on what may be obsolete tomorrow. This is especially true when they are confronted with the ceiling of COCOM regulations even as modified in 1985 which put what they can acquire some distance from the cutting edge or the state of the art. The COCOM changes now allow the 16 members to have more national autonomy in deciding on license matters. The British Department of Trade and Industry took the initiative in issuing new regulations to expedite licensing of select high technology exports to China including computers.(139)

Questions are also raised by the Chinese about actions impacting the balance of policy regarding closing the gap with advanced countries by trying to leapfrog to the forefront of technology and bypassing present day technology. Huan Zaing makes the case for the bypassing of traditional development to bring China into parity with advanced Western countries.(136)

## Market Competition

The older leadership personnel in the computerworld in many instances have been trained abroad. This has resulted in a stated preference for foreign machines. This preference is also supported by the comparative quality and reliability of foreign equipment. It is also driven by the desire to come as close as possible to accessing the technology and computer equipment which is on the cutting edge of the computer universe.

Foreign computer companies constrained by COCOM have recognized the major division in the Chinese computerworld which reflects competition beween an internal domestic computer industry and the drive to acquire the latest and most advanced equipment. These companies have also recognized the utilization by the Chinese of UN and World Bank channels to mitigate the impact of COCOM regulations. Finally they have recognized the need for a training and service infrastructure.

As a consequence foreign companies have bought into the concept of joint ventures coupled with training and service centers. This is allowing them to develop an important quasi-foreign infrastructure allowing them to obtain sales leverage and has led to the dumping in some cases of equipment that has not lived up to its expectations.

The eagerness of the Chinese to acquire equipment on the cutting edge resulted in a buying binge which produced a glut in the domestic market which then constrained production and sales of China made computers. Simultaneously this buying binge eroded foreign currency reserves. The Chinese reaction was characterized by a protectionist approach focused on increased customs duties and tightened controls of foreign exchange expenditures.

Another controlling factor helping the Chinese is the extent of their ownership in joint ventures. Examples of 50%-50% ownership are:

36

* Hewlitt-Packard and CEIEC
* Lityan Develand and Guangzhou Audio and
  Electronic Appliance Factory (177,178)

## Summary

One realistic summary of problems in the computer enterprise cites three Chinese divorces:

* Hardware divorced from software
* Processor divorced from system
* Mainframe divorced from application

However, the fundamental or core problems at the moment would appear to be lack of enough adequately trained technical personnel, precision production, the challenge of the explosiveness of the computer world, the challenging infiltration of their market through joint ventures and allied infrastructures, isolation because of vertical integration and weakness in multidiciplinary activities. Several of these factors preclude the Chinese from getting an optimum return on their computer investment.

# II. HISTORICAL DEVELOPMENT

The purpose of this section is to develop an overview covering computers, computer development, the domestic computer industry, computer imports, computer applications, and computer problems in China during 1958-1985. However, some mention is made of subsequent developments and outstanding achievements.

China, with the assistance of the Soviet Union, entered the computer world in 1958 producing its first 1st generation vacuum tube computer, the "August 1". Several years later, in 1960, the Soviet assistance ended. China was left with "self reliance", development of its own computer industry and imports. Its own computer industry was able to bring it into the 2nd generation of transistorized computers by approximately 1964. However, by 1966, at the start of the Cultural Revolution, the Soviet Union's BESEM6 was capable of 1 million ops while the Chinese computers by 1964, were capable of only 115k ops.

China, overtaken by the Cultural Revolution between 1966-76, suffered major disruptions. In spite of disruption, China was able, somehow, to remain relatively competitive with computer achievements of the Soviet Union. The Soviet Union came out with the BESEM6 in 1966, but it was not until the early 70s that the Chinese came out with the DJS11, a 3rd generation integrated circuit computer capable of 1 million ops. The gap was closing slowly, however. By 1977, the Chinese came out with the model 013, developed at the Institute of Computer Technology CAS, which was a third generation machine capable of 2 million ops as compared to the 1976 RIAD 1060 of the Soviet Union which was only capable of 1.5 million ops. Seemingly, on the surface, the gap had closed and the Chinese had gone ahead of the Soviets.

Szuprowicz (34) claimed that the reason that the Chinese were able to close the gap and forge ahead was that the Soviet Union chose to concentrate on production of R&D computers "designed to use the older IBM 360 series software". Szuprowicz hedged his position of a closed gap by stating that it was possible that much faster Soviet computers had been produced for military use. In fact, he went on to state that "there have

37

been several indications that computers with speeds between 80 and 120 million ops were under development in the Soviet Union." (34) While the Soviets were not world leaders in computer development, this limited comparison gives some indication of the competitive computer achievements of the Chinese during the Cultural Revolution, a most difficult period.

The Chinese decided to follow the Russian approach and concentrate on the development of a super computer by the military. They apparently accepted certain compromises that would dictate moving computer development toward military objectives emphasizing strategic considerations at the expense of civilian goals and a slower pace for development of computers and their applications in the civilian sector. The result has been the reported development of a Galaxy super computer by the research staff of the National University of Defense Technology in Changsha and others. This machine has been reported by the Beijing Review and China Daily as capable of more than 100 million ops .The task was assigned in May of 1978 and took approximately six years to complete. It is worth noting that in this effort China departed from strict adherence to vertical integration and involved twenty other institutes, fast tracking and importing as many foreign components as possible. Also of interest is the fact that the Chinese have brought together a 32 member national appraisal committee that certified that the computer and its supporting options were up to national standards. Attention to standards was given great support in developments of 5/7/83 with the establishment of the National Technical Committee of Standardization of Computer Information Processing. Consistent with the concerns of such a committee, the Galaxy was also examined by 95 computer experts and technicians and given an uninterrupted trial run of over 13,000 hours.(132)

Logically, there was strong military support and protection of the computer and electronic industries, and their developmental achievements during the Cultural Revolution. In spite of this, there was a discernable hiatus. One does not get reports of mass production until approximately 1973 or 1974. Even in 1973/74, there were some differences of opinion about what was going on. Cheatham (36) in 1973, for example, reported between 100 and 300 111s in all of China while Ornstein reported only 20. The DJS130, also a 3rd generation Chinese computer that became very popular, apparently got under way between 1974 -76. It was actually 1979 -80 before the words mass production appear in the literature. (37) In further support of this point of view, there was an eight year break in the reported production data of the Huadong Computer Institute (also called the East China Research Institute of Computer Technology) between the transistorized computer produced in 1965 and the IC model DJS11 also called 655 produced in 1973. (2) Szuprowicz also supports the slowdown when he reports that the total number of computers in China was 700 in 1973 and only 1000 in 1978.(34)

Certainly, after the cessation of Russian help, most of China's scientific and technical exchanges and/or cooperation, until the 70s and probably until 1978, was mainly with the governments of Asia, Africa, Latin America, and East European countries. However, as early as 1971 changes were in the making. In July, 1971, Henry Kissinger, US Security Advisor, paid a secret visit to Beijing and four days later, President Nixon stated he would visit China at Chou Enlai's invitation on a mission "to seek the normalization of relations between the two countries and as a journey of peace". Kissinger returned in October, 1971 to plan the Nixon visit which came in 1972 and included Shanghai, Hangzhou and Beijing. In spite of continuing internal turmoil in China, the change in US/China relations ushered in a new era which produced the dramatic events of normalization of diplomatic relations and China obtained a most favored nation trade status which would significantly impact the size and speed of computers that could be imported. As the Cultural Revolution wound down by 1976, there was a gradual return to normality in China. China then attempted to take stock of where it was, where it should go, and how it should go about it. This resulted in the National Science Conference on March 18, 1978, where Fang Yi spoke on the National Plan for the Development of Science and Technology (1978-1985). He had these things to say: "The eight - year outline plan draft gives prominence to the comprehensive S&T spheres....agriculture, energy, materials, electronic computers, lasers, space, high energy physics and genetic engineering."(39) Actually science and technology was one of and perhaps the most important of the Four Modernizations; Agriculture, Defense, Industry, and Science and Technology. In detail, Fang Yi said this about electronic computers: "China must make a big new advance in computer science and technology. We should lose no time in solving the scientific and technical problems in the production of large scale integrated circuits, and make a breakthrough in the technology of ultra-large scale integrated circuits. We should study and turn out giant computers, put a whole range of computers in serial production, step up study on peripheral equipment on software for computers and on applied mathematics and energetically extend the application of computers. We aim to acquire, by 1985, a comparatively advanced force in research in computer science and build a fair size modern computer industry. Microcomputers will be popularized and a giant ultra high speed computer put into operation. We will also establish a number of computer networks and data bases. A number of key enterprises will use computers to control the major processes of production and management."(39)

Approximately one year and three months later, China was reported as having 80 computer manufacturing factories. One prototype developer, the East China Research Institute of Computer Technology was staffed with approximately 1200 people including all levels. The Suzhou Computer Factory was reported in 1979, by a visiting Japanese group, as the largest and best equipped computer plant they saw. When one adds the Academy of Sciences, the former Ministry of Education and top key university computer personnel to the personnel of the 80 factories, it becomes clear that China by 1980 had a large number of personnel ranging from technicians at a semi skilled level, to skilled knowledgable theoreticians. SACI's Li Rui in suggesting that computer research institutes and main computer equipment and accessory plants allocate 30% of their skilled manpower to technical service and that the total pool was 30,000 to 40,000 (96) one can speculate that conservatively, China might have over 50,000 persons involved in the area of computer research and development, maintenance and manufacture.

The plan was to expand this labor pool as a result of training agreements reached between 1978 and 1980 with American, British, French, German, Italian, Japanese, and Yugoslavian companies. Some of the companies involved were Burroughs, Control Data Corp., Fujitsu, Hewlitt Packard, IBM, Nippon Electric, Scintrex, Sord, Sperry Univac and Unicom. UNDP and UNFPA involvement helped expand the training push. Still, those in China who knew about computers would be a privileged few.

Clearly, China was reaching out between 1978 - 80 with import orders in some cases related to or growing out of technical cooperation agreements, training agreements, protocols, contracts, and limited, and tentative joint venture efforts to accelerate achievement and response to the 1978-85 plan. Since 1978, China entered into 13 agreements on scientific and technological cooperation and numerous agreements on economic industries with the governments of Australia, Belgium, Britian, Denmark, Finland, France, Greece, Italy, Japan, Luxemberg, Norway, Sweden, United States, and West Germany. Since 1979, China actively supported and participated in the UN Intergovernmental Committee on Science and Technology for Development, the UN Center on Science and Technology for Development, as well as the UN Interim Fund on Science and Technology for Development.

Some of the S&T and economic agreements have been characterized by demonstrable quantitative sucesses - others by potential. The US, in 1979, signed not only a broad agreement for cooperation in science and technology on the occasion of Vice Premier Deng's visit, but promptly executed 13 seperate agency-to-agency agreements involving such agencies or departments as Agriculture, Commerce, Energy, Environment, Housing and Urban Development, Health and Human Services, National Aeronautics and Space Administration, and the National Science Foundation. In evaluation, the 1981 report of the State Department by Suttmeier (41) declares the US China scientific cooperation a success. Subsequently additional agreements have been executed. By 1984 twenty protocols involving 300 joint projects were in existence.(45)

If one judges the success of such broad agreements and efforts solely by the narrow criterion of a computer market share, both the US and Japan were highly sucessful. However, in contrast, France's Ministry of Industry and the 4th Ministry of Machine Building of China entered into a technology transfer pact covering cooperation in data processing systems, mini-computers, micro-processors, computers, peripherals, software and networks. Briefly, the reaction was that France had achieved both a spectacular agreement and that the agreement would preempt much of the China market. Apparently, this did not happen, primarily because of a conservative French approach concerned about the vehicle of joint ventures for which there was no adequate legal and accounting framework in China at that time. However, a French trade mission announced in 1980, $120 million of 1979 computer orders apparently not finalized by July, 1980. Then in an article by Mr. J.M. Duke Sterling, Honeywell Information Systems, (HIS) Vice President and General Manager, Honeywell International said that, " it makes sense for Honeywell Bull to enter the China market because China has established lines of credit with France, whereas US funding still has to be worked out."(42) (Honeywell Bull was 47% owned by HIS).

In the arena of joint ventures, in spite of French conservativism and a variety of problems, there was action. Japan with Fujitsu, Sord, Toshiba, Unicom Automation, and others, the US with Hewlitt Packard, Honeywell, and Sperry Univac, Britain with Marconi Avionics, France with Honeywell Bull, Sperry and Thompson CSF and even Yugoslavia actively pursued negotiations. China clearly was attempting to build its computer industry, expand its related technical manpower base, reduce production costs, obtain technology transfer and gear up for export of certain kinds of computer equipment. China also formed the International Trust Investment Company (CITIC) to buttress this effort.

Meanwhile, even though the Chinese were hard at work with impressive domestic achievements, the computer world had made great strides during the period 1966-76 and the Chinese were at a serious disadvantage. Some of their more impressive and projected achievements are listed.

* Szuprowicz reported China making its own ICs in 1973
* Kobyashi, President of Nippon Electric, told the press that China
  was producing high capacity LSIs (10K transistor elements
  compared to 12k US and Japanese elements) at the Beijing
  Semi-Conductor Plant in 10/75
* Szuprowicz reported rapid strides in micro- processor work as a
  result of use of LSI work being done at Qinghua University in
  1977
* East China Research Institute of Computer Technology built the
  first large IC computer capable of five million ops in 1979
* China is reported to have developed a strategy for the role of
  computers in China (the strategy designed by six people, four
  MIT trained) in 1979. This seems to be somewhat questionable.
*China developed a small electronic computer capable of responding
  to 100 voice commands in 1979 (by 1980---400)
* The Chinese Academy of Sciences reported that the Shanghai
  Institute of Metallurgy developed an ECL 1024 bit random
  access memory which was up to world standards in 1979
* Shanghai Radio Plant #14 and others produced the first set of

electronic minis for industrial automation manufacture in 1979
* The price of the DJS130 workhorse was cut in half in 1979
* The National University of Defense Technology is reported to
 have developed during 1983 to 1986 a computer capable of 100
 million ops as well as a preprocessor and simulator. This
 machine is essentially an advanced 4th generation computer
* CAS expects to have a super computer capable of 20 million ops
 by 1987

It is interesting to note that in spite of the 1978 National Science Conference computer posture of Fang Yi, the Chinese Academy of Sciences and the National Science Foundation did not add Basic Computer Science or Information Science to the Fields of Cooperation until 1982 and it took some behind the scenes prodding on both sides. If a general assessment is attempted from the vantage point of 10/84 it becomes clear that China, in spite of the cited 1978 statements of Fang Yi, had not given a real broad-based top priority to the entire Chinese computer world. By 1985 the balance between military and civilian priority appeared to be undergoing modification.

Subsequent statements made by Premier Zhao Zi Yang at the Sixth National People's Congress in 1983 relating to computer area goals and objectives were contained in the sixth and seventh five year plans. The S&T plan for the year 2000 concerning the formation of a computer leading group headed by Vice Premier Wan Li signaled an interest for change. However, China Daily reported (129) that Jiang Zemin, former Minister for Electronics Industry, stated "The Ministry will give priority to the development of electronic goods used by the military and let the production of those goods stimulate civilian production." The question then becomes, how much has Zhao signaled? The China Letter in August, 1983 reported: "China's computer industry's development is far behind that of the modern advanced countries. Existing development programs have been designed to support military progress, research institutes and other highly specialized needs". Wang Xinggang, researcher at the CAS Institute of Computer Technology says that early development strategy was based on erroneous assumptions which still exist.(106) The question immediately arises, has Wang's position been cleared. The answer, given the system and the still uncertain status of intellectuals, is probably yes. This probably is confirmed by the changes contained in 1985 reforms. Therefore, Wang's recommendations assume considerable significance:

* Develop a sound strategy for computer development based on
 market forecasting that pinpoints priorities, economic benefits
 and social effects.
* Concentrate on computer services and software since China can be
 most competitive quickly at a relatively low cost.
* Look to developing countries for sales opportunities (106)

Wang's criticism of the existing system is summarized in the following statement,"Development was based on an overemphasis on hardware and a neglect of software; an overemphasis of R&D and a neglect of processes and education; and an overemphasis of applications testing with a neglect of applications effectiveness. The result has been unreliable computers, incomplete configurations and difficulty in use and maintenance." (106)

In spite of the somewhat differing points of view of Zemin and Zi Yang, regarding achievements, and projected achievements, it is possible to identify a list of pre-1980 problems and problem areas, constraining the achievement record, some of which were apparent in Fang Yi's remarks at the National Science Conference in 1978:

* The Cultural Revolution's disruption (1966- 76 computer R&D stoppage) while there were major advances in the computer world outside China
* The uncertain status of academic-intellectual-computer personnel
* The post 1978 economic downturn and lack of foreign exchange negatively impacting acquisition or importation. There has recently been dramatic change in this area.
* The importance of the military in the China computer world
* The need for technically trained manpower given the magnitude of the Chinese computer effort; the need exhibited in China's interest in training agreements affiliated with purchase orders
* Software and peripheral deficiencies
* Weakness in precision manufacturing
* The lack of serial and mass production and the lack of standardization
* Too much emphasis on one-of-a-kind imports and prototype development
* The slow development of VLSICs
* The absence of time sharing and actual networking
* Poor computer utilization due to considerable down time and inadequate maintenance
* Lack of significant incentives in the development system
* Lack of substantial US and Japanese (computer leaders) involvment until 1978
* Modernization of the telephone and switchgear telecommunications system
* Purchase slowdowns and access ceilings caused or set by COCOM regulation and pre 1980 US policy
* Absence of World Bank credit prior to 1980
* Substantial end user impact of the military on design and priorities which has seen a decline by 1985
* Continued lack of coordination between research, development, manufacturing and end users

Prior to attempting a general evaluation of where China stood in the computer world in the time frame of 1978-80, three additional areas need to be examined. First, how had China progressed with application of computers? Second, what was the total computer inventory, in aggregate numbers, that existed in China? Third, how did China compare to the cutting edge of the computer world?

Between 1977 and 1986 there were reports of the application of computers in many areas. Appendix C lists many of these areas.

In 1986 the pattern of orders indicates a growing emphasis on application to the banking world, a continued emphasis on geologic data research and automation of offshore oil fields for the petroleum and mineral resources areas, construction design and product management, automotive traffic control (149) and with a new application emerging in the area of labor safety.

The maximum consistent China inventory figure reported through 1980, by three different sources, was a total of 2615 computers of which 2297 were Chinese and 318 were imported. By 1986 the inventory had risen to a total of 7000 computers excluding micros.

Most estimates of the gap between China and the cutting edge of the computer world placed China in 1980, ten to fifteen years behind in computer science, computer hardware, technology manufacture and development. In peripherals and software, the verdict was more like 15 years. All of this is rather interesting as Szuprowicz (73) cited Wang Zhen, then Minister of the former 4th Ministry of Machine Building as stating in a 1977 interview, that he considered China's progress in computers adequate. Szuprowicz hypothesizes that what Zhen meant was that the then current computer achievements were adequate to meet short term objectives. Measured against Fang Yi's objectives, the Zhen point of view would not seem wholly satisfactory to the Chinese. Our conclusion is that in 1987 China is still ten to fifteen years behind the world leaders in almost all aspects of the computer spectrum except for the area of Chinese character I/O.

In summary of where the Chinese were in the computer world in 1986, one approach is to measure their progress against Fang Yi's 1978-85 computer objectives in light of the fact that they have completed the seven year plan, and against the cutting edge of the computer world at large. Fang Yi's objectives were:

* To quickly solve the scientific and technical problems in the industrial production of both large and ultra large scale integrated circuits
* To develop giant ultra high speed computers and put them into operation
* To put a range of computers into serial production and to popularize micros
* Step up the study of peripherals and software
* Extend the application of computers

* Expand the technical manpower base or computer work force
* Build a fair sized computer industry
* Establish computer networks and data bases

The record shows that China was making its own ICs as early as 1973. The Japanese reported in 1975 that China was producing high capacity LSIs. Szuprowicz reported in 1977 that the Chinese were making rapid strides in their work in microprocessors resulting from the use of LSIs. Therefore, it is clear that the Chinese were hard at work on circuitry even before the March, 1978 statements of Fang Yi. There is even one citation in Aeronautical Knowledge on ultra large scale integrated circuits indicating that there was some evidence of large scale work.(44) However even as late as 1985 reports persisted of low yield and consequent high cost on some of the more sophisticated items.(130) In regard to the development of giant ultra high speed computers, three data points are worth mentioning: the existence of a two million ops computer, a five million ops computer built by the East China Research Institute of Computer Technology, and a report in January, 1980, that China expected to have a super computer capable of 20 million ops using high speed emitter coupled logic circuits in the near future. To date, there has been no confirmation of this but our understanding is that this project has been abandoned because of competition that represented duplication of effort by MEI and CAS. This resulted in the 757, a 10 million ops vector computer developed by CAS. One, two five and ten million ops computers are in operation. At least one 100 million machine, one ten million machine, one five million machine, a two million machine and no more than two or three one million machines represent their most powerful machines. As for a range of computers in serial production, the Chinese had by October, 1980, two mini computer series, The DJS 100 series consisting of the DJS110, 120, 130, and 140, and the DJS180 series consisting of the DJS183, 184 and 185. In addition, the medium sized general purpose mini DJS200 series consisting of the 210, 220, 240, and 260 was just starting.

Worth noting at this point, because of serialization and standardization problems, is one of the first pieces of evidence of government action. Mr. Yoshioka, Executive Director, Japanese Electronic Industry Development Association, in an October, 1980, report in the China Newsletter, stated in reference to the PRC " the Central Government apparently is pushing a program for national standardization and has set up a committee to decide on uniform specifications for the series." An article in The Standardization Journal, #8 of 1983, contained a report about the National Technical Committee of Standardization for Computer Information Processing, established in Beijing on May, 7, 1983, indicating growing concern and emphasis in this area. By 1984 the Chinese had established a Leading Group for the Invigoration of the Electronics Industry.

As indicated, 1979-80 is the first year the words, mass production, happened to be used, indicating an understanding for the need of a real shift from an emphasis on one of a kind prototype production. However, in analysis, it would not appear that any substantial mass production is underway. Clearly, the emphasis on expansion of the computer world, including the study of peripherals and software, is evidenced in the training and joint venture agreements mentioned earlier. Certainly, popularization and application of computers has been reported to move rapidly and widely if not always efficiently. Application has been afflicted by poor maintenance, service and other problems impacting computer development. However, some corrective action was appearing in 1983 with incentive systems for developers related to marketing. This action has become intensified in 1985.

To facilitate resolution of some of the problems impacting application and to optimize approaches, a computer applications research center was formed under the MEI. This research center has subsequently become the China Computing Systems Engineering Corporation.(130) Evidence also exists in the nature of joint venture agreements that China is in a hurry to develop a fair sized computer industry. However, to support such an industry, there has to be greater national computer literacy which is contingent on rapid recovery from the disastrous impact of the Cultural Revolution on the universities, solution of the problem of Chinese character representation, a larger computer work force, and a growing number of end users. Szuprowicz reflected optimism on this latter point. From the point of view of the record of applications that are underway and the pending UN training and development efforts that are underway, it would appear that Szuprowicz's optimism may be correct and that progress is being made toward developing a fair sized computer industry. Other evidence to support this is found in reports about joint assembly production efforts aimed at export. These efforts take advantage of low cost, high profits and meet the Chinese desire to build foreign reserves. The only real evidence of moves towards networks and establishment of data bases are contained in an article covering a conference on chemical applications of computer software which contained the following language: "at the meeting, this country's first cooperative network for computerized medical use software was set up with 38 units participating,"(6) and in the reports of the Beijing Document Center and the International Economic Cooperation Center for Information Processing, which involved UN support, and the projected census project. Another data point is the Chinese Academy of Social Science's, Yan Shan Corporation of Beijing, and its role in planning, implementing, and coordinating a nationwide computer system to compile, retrieve, and store statistical data. Therefore, evidence exists that network and data base efforts are being planned and are in an early developmental stage in spite of the constraints of limited manpower and a poor telecommunication system. Roughly, three years into the eight year plan, it is hard to judge how much substance there is in some of these reports. While various kinds of progress are being made and contracts have been awarded to the Swedes and French to install new telephone systems in Beijing and Tianjin, no effective networking will appear until a combination of new long lines, new modern switch gear, microwave stations in quantity, and satellite links are available.

Clearly, a major effort, but not a total top priority effort, was underway to respond to all of Fang Yi's stated 1978-85 objectives. Unfortunately, the effort has been marred by some fundamental errors such as importing without adequate numbers of personnel to operate and maintain existing computer structure, counter productive oscillations in import structure and control, procrastination over simple things like computer environmental conditions and persistent use of papertape. However, most significant of all, was the enormous competitive disadvantage which confronted China as it started its 1978-85 year plan. Approximately ten years earlier, China's 013 computer was capable of 2 million ops while the Control Data 7600 built in the US was capable of 100 million ops. By 1978, the best machine China had was capable of 5 million ops. By 1983 China reported having a 100 million ops machine.

By 1986 CAD/CAM was becoming one of the more popular computer techniques being used in China. Most of the equipment for this purpose was imported from the US or Japan. Installations were to be seen in universities, research institutes and software development organizations.

Two key questions arise: (1) Has the Cultural Revolution irretrievably destroyed China's competitive position in the computer world? (2) Was the momentum of computer achievement in the 4th and 5th generation computers elsewhere in the world such that China would be unable to compete sucessfully? The answers to these questions emerge in a variety of places throughout this work.

It is our conclusion that in the development of the computerworld China has arrived at a phase of exploratory transition characterized by tension between the drive to access and import versus the drive to develop a domestic computer industry.

# III. SUBSTRUCTURES OF THE CHINA COMPUTER WORLD

The Chinese in developing their computers have tried to serve four functions as shown in Figure 3.1 These functions have given rise to a complex structure that is governed by both political and technological leaders. It is not difficult to identify major players in the computer structure such as the State Council, The State Planning Commission, the State Scientific and Technological Commision, The State Education Commission, The National Defense Council, the Ministry of Electronics Industry, the Ministry of Foreign Economic Relations and Trade, and the Academy of Sciences and pertinent subsets or organizations. However, it is a difficult, if not an impossible task to identify those that manage, operate or speak for China's computer industry. If there is a small core of "Grey Eminences," one might speculate about people such as: Li Peng, Premier, member of the State Council and Director of the Leading Group for the Invigoration of the Electronics Industry; Fang Yi, member of the Political Bureau of the Central Committee of the CCP and member of the State Council; Zhang Aiping, Minister, Ministry of National Defense; Li Zhaoji, advisor to the Leading Group, and Vice Chairman CEIEC; Lu Dong, Deputy Director, Leading Group, Chairman, State Planning Commission; Song Jian, Deputy Director, Leading Group, Chairman SSTC; Zhao Dongwan, Deputy Director Leading Group, Minister of MLP; Nie Li, Deputy Director, Leading Group, Vice Chairman, of S&T Committiee NDSTIC; Li Tieying, Deputy Director of the Leading Group, Minister MEI; Li Xianglin, Director, Office of the Leading Group for Electronics; Tang Bingwu and Jiang Xueguo, Deputy Directors of the Office of the Leading Group; Jiang Zemin, former Minister of MEI; Lu Jiaxi, President, Chinese Academy of Sciences; Zhou Peiyuan, member of the Presidium, CAS, former President of Beijing University, and Head of CAST; Xie Xide, member Presidium, CAS, and President, Fudan University; Xu Kong Shi, formerly Deputy Director, Institute of Computer Technology and currently Director, Institute of Software Research CAS, Chen Hou-Wang, Professor, Changsha Institute of Technology, NUDT; Yan Dong Sheng of the CAS and member of the Leading Group; Li Yu-en,

49

50

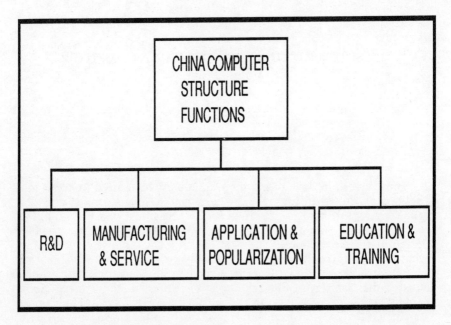

Figure 3.1 Computer Structure

Chief Engineer, National Bureau of Standards and Lee Chen, President, National Committee of Standardization of Computer and Information Processing.

This group of people by virtue of position, stroke, function and responsibility cut across most of the ten areas identified in the overall structure. There are also other organizations and people that are intimately involved in the China computer world. For example, those involved in the process of clearance of computer import purchases: "Orders must be approved by the State Planning and Economic Commission and by the Ministry of Foreign Economic Relations and Trade."(12) The overall structure, if one can judge just by the area of "import", suffers from oscillations. In import, there were definite oscillations from centralization to decentralization. For example, in late 1981 there was a sharp reversal in the trend toward decentralization in control of importation of high technology. The reasons for this were: (1) the confusion caused by decentralization; (2) loss of control of foreign exchange (late 1981 all overseas foreign exchange accounts were closed); and (3) loss of control of proper preparation for imported equipment. (46) This was in reaction to the type of decentralization initiated in Fujian Province in 1980.(47) Reaction culminated in a requirement that from minis up, there is a need for approval of the State Science and Technology Commission's Computer group and the Ministry of Electronics Industry. Recently, micro imports have also been restricted. In order to be able to import a micro, need must be proved as well as lack of availability in China.

Another example of an oscillation is contained in a Della Bradshaw article (48), which reports: "Approval of joint ventures between Chinese organizations and overseas companies originally could only be given by the central government. Now, however, they can be given by local government." Clearly, this is not consistent with the new centralization move in the importation area. A series of questions arises. Does any group really know what is going on? How and where is coordination achieved, if it is? How can orderly, cohesive, well planned change as opposed to random oscillatory change occur within this diverse, unwieldy structure?

In an effort to seek answers to these questions, it will be helpful to examine in detail the substructure.

Government Substucture (See Figure 3.2)

China's State Council.

*China International Trust and Investment Corporation (CITIC)
*The Leading Group for the Invigoration of the Electronics
    Industry.

The State Planning Commission

*Representation on Leading Group for Invigoration of the
    Electronics Industry
*The National Economic Information Center Computer Center
*The Provincial Planning Commission's Provincial Computer
    Centers

The State Science and Technology Commission

*Leading Group representation
*Institute of Scientific and Technical Information (ISTIC)
    ISTIC's tasks include:
        * The collection and arrangement of domestic and foreign
          science and technology information
        * Leading Group representation
        * Translation and reporting on science and technology
        * Documentation service.
            ISTIC has initiated active research on computerized
            searching and machine translation.(49) Several offices of
            this organization should be mentioned. They are, The
            Office of Computers, The Office of Information Methods

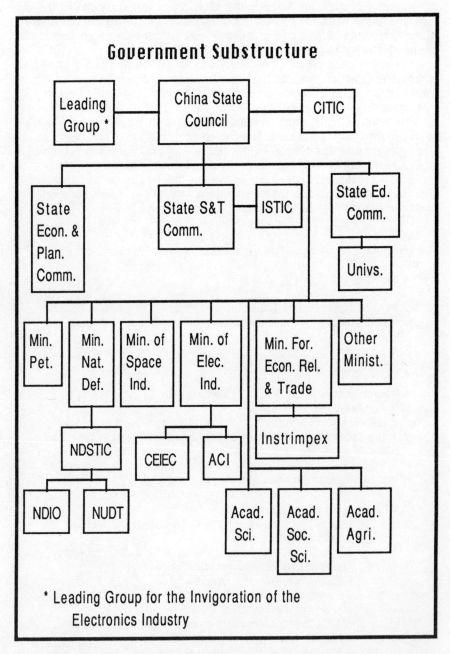

Figure 3.2 The Govenment Substructure Relating to Computers

Research, and the Department of Information Research.
The activities of ISTIC cover sixty three countriesand fifty
three additional international organizations.
*Science and Technology Information Center (97)

## Ministry of Electronics Industry

*Leading Group representation
*Administration of Computer Industry (formerly State
    Administration Computer Industry (SACI))
*Radar Industry Bureau
*Communications Broadcast and Television Industries Bureau
*Electronic Computer Industry Bureau
*Electronic Components and Devices Industry Bureau
*China Electronics Import/Export Corporation (CEIEC)
*China Corp.of Electronic Devices Industry
*China Electronic Materials and Equipment Corp.
*China Communications Engineering Corp.
*China Computer Technical Services Corp. (CCTSC)
    Branch operations
*China Software Technique Corp.
*China Computer Machine Room Eng'g Corp.
*China Computer Systems Engineering Corp. (probably also
    known as Research Institute of Computer System Engineering)
*East China Research Institute of Computer Technology
*North China Institute of Computer Technology
*Other Research Facilitites and Universities
    Chengdu Institute of Radio Technology
    Beijing Information Engineering Institute
    Broadcast and Electroacoustics Institute
    Semiconductor Research Institute in Shijiazhuang, Hebei
    Semiconductor Technology Research Institute in Changsha
        These five institutions have been confirmed in discussion
        with Gu Duren and another source.(2,70,175)
*Micro-computer Information Network (Shanghai group, and
    others)

## Ministry of National Defense

*National Defense Scientific and Technological Industry
    Commission (linked to CITIC)
*National University of Defense Technology
*National Defense Industries Office
*PLA's General Logistics Office
*Academy of Military Science and research institutes
*Institute for Strategic Studies
*Leading Group representation

## Ministry of Foreign Economic Relations and Trade

*International Economic Center, Information Processing and Training
*China National Instrument Import/Export Corporation (Instrimpex or CNIIEC)
*China National Technical Import Corporation

## Other Government Computer Centers

*Three computer centers of the Ministry of Petroleum
*Western Yunan Earthquake Center and two other computer centers of the State Siesmological Bureau

## Ministry of Space Industry

*Chinese Academy of Space Technology research institutes

## National Institute of Meteorology

## Provincial Computer Centers

*Each province has its own computer center (for example, Anhui, Hebei, Heilongjiang, Liaoning, and Sichuan and even autonomous regions such as Nei Mongol)

## Municipal Centers

*Beijing, Shanghai and Tianjin Computer Centers
*Beijing Municipal Computer Center also known as the Beijing Center for International Economic Information

## State Commission of Education

*Representation on Leading Group
*Ten leading university computer centers
*Top key university computer centers
*Other university computer centers

## Chinese Academy of Sciences (CAS)

*Computer Center
*Institutes of Computing Technology (Beijing and Shenyang)
*Institute of Software
*Institute of Computer Application
*Scientific Instruments Factory
*Oriental Scientific Instrument Import/Export Corporation

## The Chinese Academy of Social Sciences

*Yan Shan (Swallow Mountain) Science and Technology
Corporation. This organization was reported as being
"resposible for planning implementing, and coordinating a
nationwide computer system to compile, retrieve, and move
statistical and scientific data." (38,50,51). Its immediate task is
to select an approach for processing Chinese character texts.
Eventually, it will provide technical support to the entire
government. The corporation reports directly to CASS and
administers the Beijing Computing Applications Research
Center, now known as the Computer Application Research
Center, Yan Shan Corporation. It was reported in 1984 that this
organization has approached foreign firms for military or high
technology imports.(182)

## Chinese Academy of Agricultural Science

*Computerized Test Center of the Institute of Pedology
and Fertilizers (52)

## China International Engineering Consulting Corp.

*CIECC Beijing (53)

There are many issues confronting this substructure. The following
list identifies those that are of major importance.

* Coping with tension of acquisition and imports versus
development of a domestic computer industry
* Shall China produce for secondary needs and import for critical
needs within the constraints of COCOM or be wholly self
reliant?
* Phasing of catch up or development of competitve capability
and strategy.
US role
Foreign role
Technology acquisition and transfer
* Elimination of overlap and redundancy
* Allocation of resources and development of a balanced system
* Centralization vs. decentralization
* Standards
* Development of a modern telecommunications system
* Reassurance of intellectuals
* Manpower development
* Increased or improved priority status
* Development of incentive systems

* Commitment to regional centers
* The impact of the military on computers
* Vertical integration
* Automation vs. displacement

In regard to elimination of overlap and redundancy, there is virtually no evidence of an effort to accomplish this, or to conserve and find new resources. If anything, it appears that redundancy is entirely acceptable. In addition, there was no evidence of a concerted effort to optimize a return on the investment in the Chinese computer world until the emergence in 1983 of an incentive system. Responses to the issue include work on the standards problem, the computer down time problem and the emergence of computer corporations to provide software and service.

Evidence of allocation of monetary resources based on a management science approach related to functions or to clear prioritization of substructure importance is missing. The functions referred to are; R&D, manufacturing and service, applications and popularization, and education and training. There is no discernable approach to balancing resource allocation between military and civilian domestic production and importation of equipment that is domestically available or can be domestically produced. However, in spite of tension a decision related to commitment to foreign imports has been achieved, and also a decision to reach out for help through the UN, the World Bank and cooperative and joint venture agreements which involve Chinese matching funds which could lead to a short term negative impact on the development of the domestic computer industry.

A systematic approach to technical manpower allocation on a functional or prioritized substructure basis seems lost in the mysteries of the Bureau of Science and Technology Personnel. A decision impacting this in a general way was the decision to increase from 5% to 13% the input into higher education from the middle schools' graduating classes of 1982-83. Further changes may occur as a result of the educational reforms of 1985. Some improvement was apparent in 1986 in such organizations as the North China Institute of Computer Technology but at the same time Epsom the Japanese computer company is attempting to sue the Industrial Development Service Co. in Shenzen over their inability to procure satisfactorily skilled workers.(143) On the supply side displacement caused by automation might also improve the situation. In 1984, it was reported that the computerization of the Beijing (Shoudu) Iron and Steel Co. triggered a 7000 person reduction of the work force.

The struggle over the issue of centralization vs. decentralization has been marred by oscillations over the control posture on import and export, a slow move toward imposition of standards, and a point of view strongly supportive of vertical integration. A second issue has been decentralization of the control of factories of MEI.

The computer world strategy issue has several parts. These parts are domestic production, importation, and military considerations. Apparently, China has decided to use domestic production for secondary needs and imports for critical priority needs. Such decisions necessitated a definition of critical needs. Definition of critical needs gets involved with strategic military considerations, and mobilization of resources to optimize imports of the most advanced components and systems. The final consequence of this decision appears to be the acceptance of isolation from the cutting edge of equipment development or acquisition because of the constraints of COCOM regulations and the US export bureaucracy. Apparently, the Chinese believe that as a result of a variety of their own phased catch-up initiatives, they will become competitive by the year 2000. In the course of catch-up, they may plan to skip production of several generations of computers and IC's.

Military impact evidences itself in the geographic distribution of computer centers, the concept of regional and provincial centers, and allocation of computer centers to strategic endeavors, such as:

* development of a logistics strength by expediting movement of goods and people
* development of critical natural resources, specifically, coal, oil, water, and electric power, energy in general, preliminary basic computer network structure efforts, and development of some options to facilitate command control.

It appears that the regional/provincial center complex, while accomplishing dispersion, will exacerbate the manpower shortage problem because of increasing the demand for personnel, because of expansion of the structure and because of the planned multi-faceted roles of R&D, applications, training and service at each of these centers.

Centralization and vertical integration are closely interrelated. A former decision to isolate one structure from another; for example,The Ministry of Electronics Industry (MEI) from the Academy of Sciences and the academic world, may be undergoing change as a result of the elimination of the Ministry of Education and the emergence of the State Education Commission. The consequence of the previous decision was to eliminate or reduce horizontal interaction and insure absolute control from the top. Vertical integration stood in the way of interaction between factories and end users of domestically produced computers and caused the emergence of some 1500 in-house hardware service stations.It is too soon to ascertain with certainty whether the educational reforms of 1985 will place all universities under the new State Education Commission or continue to leave some to report to various ministries.

Automation vs. displacement is a subtle unrecognized long-term issue which has a potential of overriding importance. Early evidence of this was seen at the Shanghai Electronic Computer Factory. See comments in Applications and Popularization Substructure section.

<u>Research and Development Substructure</u>  (See Figure 3.3)

### <u>The Chinese Academy of Sciences</u>

*The Computer Center
*The Institute of Computing Technology
*The Institute of Software  R&D
*The Technical Science Department
*Other related  Institutes and universities.

### <u>Ministry of Electronics Industry</u>

* Administration of the Computer Industry
* China Computing Systems Computing Corp.
* China Software Technique Corp.
* The North China Institute of Computer  Technology in Beijing
* East China Research Institute  of Computer  Technology
* Five other research institutes or  universities

### <u>State Education Commission</u>

### <u>Other Ministries</u>

* Other ministries  have had universities and  research and
  development institutes  under their control. For example, the
  former Third Ministry of  Machine Building now the Ministry of
  Aeronautics Industry, controlled  several major aeronautical
  educational institutions that have affiliated  institutes and labs
* The Beijing Institute of Aeronautics and Astronautics. (jointly
  with the State Education Commission.)
* The Nanjing  Institute of Aeronautics  and Astronautics
* The Northwestern Polytechnic  University in  Xian
* Inertial Guidance Research Labs near  Xian

### <u>Municipal and Provincial Computer Centers</u>

*These computer centers are also in the  development  business.

### <u>Other</u>

*Beijing Association Software Development  Center
*Beijing Institute of Software R&D.
*Shanghai Software Development Center (54)
*Hunan Electronics Research Institute
*Changsha Research Institute for  Semiconductor Technologies

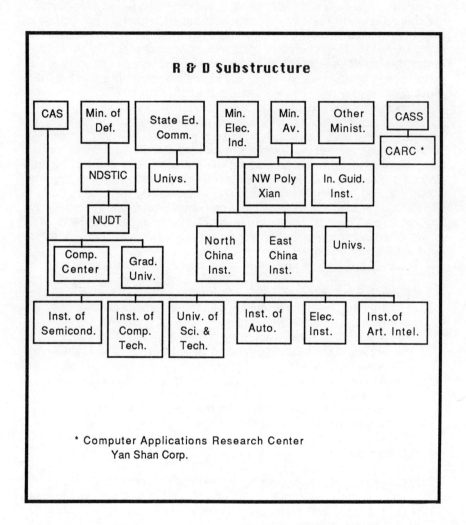

Figure 3.3  Research and Development Substructure

Also, in the R&D substructure, are the State Commission's top key universities with their computer centers. For example, Beijing University, Qinghua, Jiaotung Xian, Fudan and Jiaotung Shanghai all have centers and/or departments. Early in 1982 some sixteen universities were reported as having established computer science departments and disciplines.(55) In addition, as a result of the World Bank bid decision, fourteen new US main frames have gone to top key universities including some of the above.(56) The majority of these machines were Honeywells.

However, China had made a decision following the requests of President Emeritus Kuang of Nanjing University and others in 1983, to increase educational funding for a select group of fifty institutions of higher learning. Instead the government decided to increase funding for ten institutions destined to become top of the top key. They include Fudan, Jiaotung Shanghai, Jiaotung Xian, Beijing University, Qinghua University, and Beijing Medical College. This decision will tend to further impact in a positive manner the existing computer centers and efforts at these now very select institutions. Critical mass is being developed as well as an elitist approach. Perhaps the critical mass will lead to these institutions being the first to network computers.

There are a variety of key issues related to the R&D substructure

* Pruning redundancy
* Competing for finite resources with the education and manufacturing substructure
* Establishment of elite centers
* Mobilization of resources to take China beyond the preliminary stages of networking
* Evaluation of the time needed to arrive at the cutting edge of the computer world
* Development of a policy for allocation of CAS/NSF type program research awards
* Implementation of an entrepreneurial and incentive effort
* Production of chips, IC's and peripherals

While some redundancy may be desireable in working with finite resources, in a ball game that is distinctly catch-up, it is desireable to conserve by pruning and to mobilize the saved resources for well planned critical efforts. There is little evidence of pruning or even the recognition of it as an issue. It appears that existing redundancy will be perpetuated.

Clearly, there is competition for money, personnel and equipment with other functional areas. However, there is little evidence of a rational, orderly, managed approach to the allocation of these resources.

Elite centers will be the consequence of national policy dictating that foreign equipment be located in certain Beijing centers, certain ministries, provincial centers and selected top key universities. A recent addition to that policy focusing on Beijing, Shanghai and Guangzhou may limit geographical dispersion somewhat.

Certainly, the Chinese have recognized that total daily operating time or "up time" is much better on foreign made than domestic equipment. So it seems very likely that they have considered where their program priorities are in military, civilian, academic and university research and evaluated this in terms of geographic placement and the principle of distribution. Thus, we see World Bank computers going to top key universities and we see IBM and Wang equipment going to the provincial centers. However, questions arise, as

    * How will elite centers fare if they are in fact percieved as elite?
    * Will networks evolve around foreign equipped centers because of equipment reliability?

Evidence exists that thought is being given to networking and the cost of networking. In the course of our discussions at the Academy of Sciences and Qinghua University, as well as the universities in Chengdu, Xian, Tianjin and Shanghai, it was confirmed that this is being considered in the context of five year plans and possibly some immediate activity in Beijing. Research on networking is primarily a local activity at universities and research institutes.

The Chinese have established a goal of becoming competitive in the computer world by the year 2000. They appear to have made a decision commiting themselves to achieving this by a phased approach. This type of decision means that they plan to build the base of R&D skill, technical manpower, and knowledge, acquiring technology at a digestible rate so that at D-day and H-hour they can bypass in mass production several generations of computers and eliminate the existing gap. Clearly, this substructure has been outstandingly sucessful in developing the reported 10 million ops vector computer of the Instiute of Computing Technology, CAS, and the 100 million ops machine of the National University of Defense Technology at Changsha. Since 80 institutes and universities were involved in the development of the CAS machine and 95 experts examined the Galaxy. Perhaps evidence is developing that the impact of vertical integration will be mitigated if the priority is high enough.

## Manufacturing Substructure (See Figure 3.4)

As a result of analyzing data in a Berney article,(96) and other data in the Smith/Witzell files (2), it is possible to state that over 200 factories, institutes, and universities are involved in the production of main frames, minis, micros, and other related equipment such as peripherals, various types of printers, hole punch machines, and magnetic tape machines (see appendix A for list). In the main, these factories are located in Eastern China from Heilongjiang Province in the north , to Shanxi in the west, and Guangzhou in the south, with major concentrations occuring in and around Beijing, Shanghai and Tianjin. The capability of this domestic structure is being supplemented by the vehicle of joint ventures and various types of

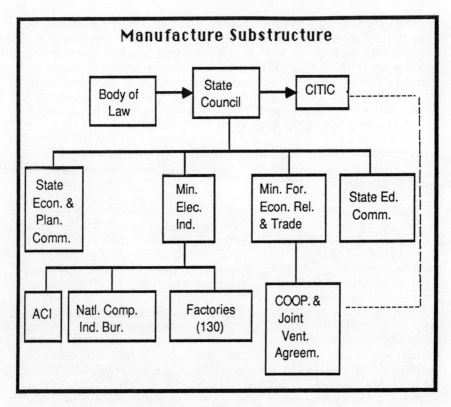

Figure 3.4 The Manufacturing Substructure

cooperative arrangements. The stage was set by the Chinese by preparing to allow 25-100% ownership of businesses by foreign firms.(57) To support this initiative, China established the China International Trust and Development Corporation (CITIC). The latest CITIC approaches and plans are revealed in a release in the February, 1982 edition of Xinhua:

CITIC TO ADOPT SPECIAL POLICIES, METHOD

> With approval of the State Council, The China International Trust and Investment Corporation (CITIC), will adopt certain special policies and economic methods on a trial basis. This was announced by Rong Yiren, Chairman and President of CITIC, at a press conference.

Thus, CITIC has become the first enterprise directly under the State Council to try out special policies in reference to the experience of Guangdong and Fujian Provinces where special policies are carried out. The highlights of these policies and methods are:

* The annual and long-term plans of CITIC will be incorporated in the State plan, and except in the case of those big projects which the State may entrust it to undertake and within the State may have funds set by the State for CITIC for a particular year, it has the right to choose medium and small projects in which it wants to invest, subject to filing a report with the proper authorities to be put on record.
* The capital of CITIC will increase from the current 200 million Yuan to 600 million Yuan. For a period of three to five years, CITIC will be exempt from turning over its profits to the State and from taxation, so that the targeted amount of capital will be reached through the accumulation of profits over the years.
* CITIC will engage in foreign exchange business. CITIC has the right to manage and use independently the foreign exchanges it borrows or earns from the enterprises in which it has invested and from other operations it engages in, and may deposit them in the Bank of China and their branches abroad or in foreign banks. CITIC may set up financial companies or other forms of organizations in cooperation with foreign monetary institutions.
* CITIC has the right to import the equipment and materials needed by the enterprises in which it has invested and the right to export their products, upon the approval of the State Administrative Commission on Import and Export Affairs.
* CITIC will recruit personnel by inviting applications and making changes in pay and bonus methods accordingly.(58)

Joint Ventures  The area of joint ventures has been one of great legal activity. This activity has produced approximately 30 laws and regulations. A sample of the laws and regulations is listed below:

* Law of China on Joint Ventures using Chinese and Foreign Investments
* Regulations of China on the Registration of Joint Ventures using Chinese and Foreign Investments
* Regulations of China on Labor Management in Joint Ventures using Chinese and Foreign Investments
* The Income Tax Law of China concerning Joint Ventures with Chinese and Foreign Investments

A comprehensive listing of the principal laws and regulations is contained in Mariana Graham's article.(40)

The October 3, 1983 issue of the Beijing Review announced that the Regulations for the Implementation of the Law of the PRC on Joint Ventures using Foreign Investment had been published the previous week and that the full text would be published on October 10, 1983.

The document contained sixteen chapters and 118 articles and covered:

* Legal position of Chinese-foreign joint ventures
* Industries eligible for joint ventures
* Application procedures
* Ways of investing
* Formation of Boards.
* Relaxation of stipulations concerning wages and incomes of foreign workers
* Exemption of Chinese-foreign joint ventures from income tax during the first two profit making years
* Other tax incentives, i.e., foreign investors will only have to pay half the income tax for years 3-5

The bottom line is to insure profit for investors. A joint venture must export a certain amount of its products to earn some foreign exchange to balance its foreign exchange payments. However, rules also provide for favorable treatment in regard to customs duty on imported machinery, equipment, etc., and self management. The general manager can be foreign or Chinese.

The Department of Science and Technology Policy of the State Science and Technology Commission stated that there were some 2100 different administrative laws or protocols that existed in China that pertained to the area of joint ventures and trade. At least 70% are under consideration for modification or elimination. The process of modification and promulgation of new law is described as complex and time consuming.(130)

In summary, according to the Beijing Review, the major area of investment has shifted from light, textile and tourist industries to high technology machine building and electronic industries with 105 Chinese-foreign joint ventures started between July 1979 and June 1983 representing an investment of $526 million of which $214 million came from foreign investors. In July 1983, Xu Pengfei, general manager of the Shanghai Trust and Investment Corporation, announced to 800 overseas business people:

* a preferential tax measure exempting from customs duties and industrial and commercial taxes, machinery, equipment and necessary goods for Chinese-foreign joint ventures;
* a reduction or exemption from industrial or commercial taxes on products manufactured for sale abroad;
* an exemption from income tax in the first two profit making years
* a 50% reduction in income tax for the next three years.

To support this, Shanghai is setting up the Minhang Development District.

Among the suggestions for incentives is one made by the Asian Studies Foundation that US industries supporting the education of Chinese graduate students in the US be given additional favorable treatment.

China Daily, in an article from Xinhua of October, 25, 1983, reported that eight contracts, four agreements, and 11 letters of intent were signed with foreign and Hong Kong businessmen at a foreign trade and technology import fair held in Tianjin on October 4 to 14, 1983. The joint ventures include cooperation and facilities for hotels, prawn breeding, chemical fabrics, steel pipe, printing and raising mushrooms. In addition, Tianjin is planning more joint ventures in its chemical, metallurgy, machine building (including automation) and electronics industries. Plans involved the International Conferences and Exhibitions Group of Lund, and the US for three trade shows in 1984, five in 1985, eight in 1986, and eight in 1987. In 1986, Wu Mingyu, Vice Minister of the State Science and Technology Commission visited the US attempting to identify problems impacting the operation of joint ventures and seeking suggestions for the improvement of Chinese law with regard to scientific and technological matters, specifically such items as patents and license agreements. Consistent with the approach of the Vice Minister, is a contract executed between Beijing University and Hamilton Brighton Inc. to sell software of a computer assisted Chinese law research system. The system includes 249 pertinent foreign economic laws and regulations in English and Chinese.

In regard to Shanghai and other cities, Chen Tantao, Chief Engineer of China Automotive Industries Corporation (CAIC) announced that AMC and Beijing Auto Works signed contracts establishing a joint venture called Beijing Jeep Corporation, Ltd., to produce jeeps of the CJ series.(43) In addition, he indicated that CAIC was negotiating with Volkswagen and Citroen for production of Shanghai sedans. He also indicated that discussions were taking place in Tianjin regarding light trucks with Daihatzu and Suzuki of Japan. Further, talks were going on in regard to joint ventures on heavy trucks with Steyr of Austria and Benz of West Germany.

Besides the special economic zones of Shenzen, the Yangzte Delta, (Minhang) and Tianjin's Tanqu there is an additional one at Xianan in Fujian Province which will also encourage joint ventures.

Basically the joint ventures tend to involve Britian,, France, Italy, Japan, Sweden, Switzerland, the US, West Germany and possibly Norway.

A sample list of some cooperative agreements and joint ventures follows (for a more comprehensive list with greater detail, including other countries, see appendix B). Also see data on the Sems mini and small computer transaction at the end of the discussion on the Maintenance and Service Substructure, for an indication of movement on the part of the French.

> Sperry Univac. Signed a cooperative contract in March 1980, loosely called a joint venture with the 4th MMB, now the Ministry of Electronics Industry and China International Trust Investment Corp. The arrangement was software oriented

with the long term objective of developing a strong computer manufacture in China. The Service Center involved in the contract was scheduled to open December 1982.

Honeywell. Signed a cooperative agreement in July 1980 to aid the Beijing wire plant in producing large scale digitals, minis (training is involved), and the transfer of the manufacture of software.

Ohio Micros. Yangtze River Industries and Ohio Micros entered into a joint venture in August 1980 for the assembly, manufacture and production of micros.

Wang. China and Wang entered into a joint venture in April 1981 to produce small computers in Nanjing with a goal of $4.5 million production in 1985. Wang executed three contracts to produce superminis and micros with MEI and others.

Hewlitt-Packard. Hewlitt-Packard and the Ministry of Electronics Industry created a distributorship (the first since 1949) in Beijing for sales and service of Hewlitt-Packard equipment. The distributorship will be an entity within the China Electronics Import/Export Corporation.In addition as a result of cooperative efforts China Hewlitt-Packard Co. Ltd. and China Electronics Import/Export Corp. and the Beijing Computer Industrial Corp. formed China's first high technology joint venture.The venture will have three functions, R & D, manufacturing and marketing. It will produce electronic testing instruments, computers and peripherals.(152)

Isotronics, Anchron Computer Products and the China Corporation for Shipbuilding Industry (CCSI). Beijing agreed to two joint ventures; establishment of a plant to manufacture printed circuit boards, and production of computer components and subassemblies in a CCSI facility for shipment to Anchron, an Isotronics subsidiary.

Santec Corporation. Santec Corporation of Amherst, New Hampshire and Nanjing Telecommunication Works formed a jointly owned company in June 1983. Santec International will do research and development on helping Chinese business use computers on a larger scale. The joint firm will also produce and market computers.

Kingtai Co. Ltd. and Wenfo International and Beijing Municipal S&T Development and Exchange Center's Software Dept. #2. Establish Beijing-Yunke Computer Service Center

A Hong Kong company and Beijing #1 Machine Tool Plant. Signed a contract to purchase and manage a numerically controlled machine tool company located in the US.

A Japanese electric company and China Electronics Technical Import Co. Signed an agreement in Feb. 1985, to produce 16 bit micros. The production company will be the North China Terminal Equipment Co.

Burroughs Corp., Yunnan Provincial Import/Export Corp., Yunnan Electronic Equipment Factory and Beijing Everbright Industrial Corp. signed a contract in Jan. 1985 for the assembly, distribution and maintenance of B20 and B25 micros for small business.(166)

Olivetti (US) and NA (HK) and Fujian Computer Corp. formed the Bailing-Olivetti Computer Corp. in August 1985 to manufacture 100,000 micros a year.

Labtam Int. Pty. Ltd. ( Australia) and CAS. Formed a joint venture in October 1985 to develop a 32 bit UNIX prototype computer using Chinese and English software.

Syntone Advanced Computer Technology Co. Ltd. A new model of an all Chinese joint venture formed by two units of CAS and the Haidan New Technology Co. The joint venture has sales, software development, production and maintenance service departments.(163)

China Computer Technical Service Corp. and K.C. Ltd. of Japan. A Sino-Japanese software joint venture opened in Kobe, Japan, in July 1984. (179)

Access to the internal electronics market tends to be limited to importing semi finished products for assembly.(146) However in 1984 China faced with the position of being overbought in micros stated that foreign computer manufacturers would be allowed a share of China's domestic market in return for introducing sophisticated technology and management skills. The Japanese put it more bluntly stating that the Chinese government was advancing a plan to suspend import of computers from foreign manufacturers that are reluctant to transfer their technology.(171, 172)

Production Two different reports placed in juxtaposition give some idea of the difficulty of estimating accurately what the expanding production capability of this manufacturing structure really is. The first report has China's growing computer industry production reported as being between 500 and 800 large computers annually with 7300 accessory units; (59) while the second report has one particular plant, the Fujian Computer Plant, reported as producing 5000 computers annually by 1979 with a reported output of 300,000 by 1981.(60) This seems very unlikely, when given a rather optimistic projection for the factories listed in appendix A, China should be producing at maximum a package of 1000 large, medium, and small computers, not including micros on an annual basis. Li Rui's report of late 1982 would seem much more reliable. At that time, he reported China as currently having a production capacity of 500 large, medium, and small sized computers and 500 micros annually. He also reported a January to September, 1982 production surge of large, medium and small computers. The 160 computers produced in the surge reflected a 62% increase in production over the previous year for the same time period while a surge of 520 micros reflected a 150 increase for the same time period. He set several goals; a 1985 production level of 1000 large, medium and small computers and 10,000 micros and single board computers; and a 1990 annual production level of 1800 large, medium and small computers plus 40,000 micros and single board computers.(10) Therefore, between 1983 and 1986, with steadily increasing capacity and production and the operation of some of the joint venture plants, along with others coming on line, there should be a significant increase in annual production but not of the magnitude suggested by Li Rui.

In this substructure the issues can be summarized as:

* Competition for resources
* Standards
* Precision and mass production
* Profits
* Product costs
* Production for export
* Encouraging foreign export
* Technology acquisition and transfer
* Elite factory groups
* Price differential between domestic and foreign computer parts

Competition for resources is a common issue impacting all four functional areas; research and development; manufacturing and service; application and popularization; and education and training.

Standards are critical in the manufacturing process and only recently have they been addressed as an issue by the formation of a computer standards group at a high level. The National Technical Committee of Standardization for Computer and Information Processing was established in Beijing on May 7, 1983. Lee Chen is president of the committee. The committee is controlled by the National Standards Bureau and others. It is the 30th committee established by the Bureau, which has worked on computer standardization since the middle 70s and there have been more than ten international standardization meetings related to networking, digital communication, software, security of data, etc. There have been 32 national standardization meetings involving such areas as program language-Algol, Basic, Fortran, and machine language, communication using seven digit characters with non-punched cards, etc.(131) The responsibilities of this committee include:

* adoption of international standards and developing related
    feasible plans
* developing plans for standardization research
* gearing national standards to the needs of China
* establishing a mechanism to review design of external devices
    and quality of magnetic tape
* coordination of involved departments
* control of a number of branch technical committees and
    development of a single group of experts
* collecting and disseminating international standardization data
    which has implications for uniform production, machining, mass
    production, and compatibility of peripherals and software.

The Chinese have made some sucessful efforts to reduce the costs of computers. The key to significant cost reduction is mass production. Price and reliability add up to sucessful competition in the world market. The Chinese are looking at a portion of this world market, a computer portion in which they can compete. An example is their ability to export the Great Wall. They are looking at potential profits which they can use to strengthen their computer effort.

However, as indicated in the coverage given to CITIC cooperation and joint ventures, the manufacturing substructure is looking for a major boost from the foreign sector in helping to expand the factory base, acquire technology, and tune-up sophisticated digestive capabilities to help develop an elite foreign trained cadre of technical people for factories.

China Market (43), contains an article which reveals plans to build a large integrated circuit industrial base in Wuxi. In support of the point of obtaining a major boost from the foreign sector, the article closes with the language, " We shall invite foreign experts to come to China to give guidance, engage in cooperative production with foreign enterprises or set up joint electronic monitors using Chinese and foreign investments." Unfortunately, this base has been less than sucessful; although sophisticated technical equipment was installed, technical and managerial competence was not.

Maintenance and Service Substructure
    (see Figure 3.5)

The China Computer Technical Service Corporation was established in 1980. Its parent organization was the State Administration of the Computer Industry (SACI) now known as the Administration of the

Computer Industry and which is part of the Ministry of Electronics Industry. The purpose of the Computer Technical Service Company is to centralize management of maintenance and service, the management of supply of accessories, and the management of technical training in computers and programming.(38)   Chen Liwei, Chief Engineer, ACI called for the consolidation and extension of technical services into a comprehensive nationwide network. In order to accomplish this, 35% of the total computer oriented staff in China would have to be allocated to technical service in the next ten years.(160)   The efforts of this substructure were focused in major cities with other branch units in provinces. A decision was reported that would lead to spreading the network throughout all China. According to Sigurdson the maintenance initially will be limited to minis. (32)   Actually there are twenty five service centers across the country. In addition, supplementing this, some ninety computer factories have established technical service departments.(59)   Another source subsequently indicated that because of the slow development of service centers, some 1500 organizations have developed their own in-house hardware maintenance and application software development personnel.(63)   The answer to the question, "are the 90 included in the 1500 " is not clear.

These efforts involve a significant commitment of manpower and stretch an already scarce commodity. This pressure for manpower was adressed in a 1983 move that restructured secondary education, making 40% of the senior middle schools into vocational schools. However, this action by itself is not adequate to meet the growing demand for service support personnel in spite of the fact that China was reported in April of 1985 to have 20,000 people working in this area.(157)   A significant change has occured. No longer is the factory producing the computer taking the position with the end user that once the machine was delivered " you are on your own". The earlier factory position, along with the slow development of service centers, drove the emergence of in-house hardware maintenance groups into 1500 organizations, and it raised the question of personnel allocation and the most productive use of personnel.

Also associated with this substructure was the network of approximately thirty provincial, autonomous regions and municipal centers. Some of these were started in the mid-70s with operations begining in 1976. For example, this was the case with the Nei Mongol Center which was later upgraded and tasked with coordinating the entire region's computer applications. It also equated or made equal the functions of research and service.(64)

These domestic efforts have been complemented by various requirements of computer sales contracts, joint ventures and cooperative agreements. For example, the purpose of the newly established Hewlitt-Packard distributorship was to put the company on market site and to put it into a position of servicing and maintaining its equipment. Different, but bearing on service and maintenance, IBM Japan, Ltd. was reported to have a PRC Development Department responsible for operational support of

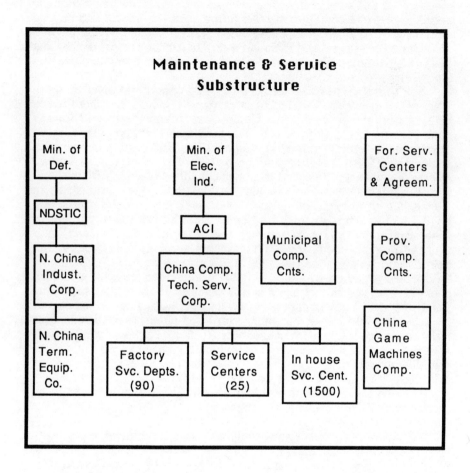

Figure 3.5  The Maintenance and Service Substructure

business activities in China.

The comprehensive nature of the Honeywell agreement, virtually a joint venture, will undoubtedly lead to training of Chinese to strengthen the maintenance and service effort. Since this agreement calls for the ultimate establishment of a computer manufacturing plant, the impact will be long term. It won't be an arrangement to train a limited number of Chinese in a short period to operate and maintain a certain package of equipment that has just been sold to China. In addition, Sperry Univac is about to open its second computer service center.(12)

The United States has not been the only country involved in these kinds of arrangements. Two recent cases; one Australian, the other French, help support the point that the Chinese are augmenting, with foreign commitments linked to joint ventures, their technical computer base by developing a foreign trained contingent. The first case, a cooperative agreement between Datamax and the Metallurgical Research Institute of Beijing, involved an agreement to manufacture the Datamax 8000 in China with Datamax agreeing to establish an electronic research institute in Guangzhou to market and maintain the 8000. The French transaction involved Sems and is somewhat different. Sems has trained two groups of Chinese personnel who have returned home to operate the Huanan (South China) Computer Company and the Guangzhou Computer Factory. The objective is to produce the HN-3000 minicomputers of the Solar 16 family, the highest grade of which is the 16/75 which can do over a million operations per second. Its maximum storage capability is 2048 kilobytes. In the end, the computer company now under construction will be able to produce not only minis, but other small computers as well, and give technical advice and render repair service.(65,66) The production line will have a capacity of 400 units per year, which can be expanded to 1200 per year. Still another example is the export to China by Syseca Co. in 1985 of a SOCRATE/CLIO DBMS software system.(157)

The central or critical problem for this substructure is obtaining enough technically trained manpower to:

* make certain that existing equipment recieves optimum use
* down time is minimized
* the overall computer structure is operated as efficiently as possible

Some of the issues impacting the Maintenance and Service substructure are:

* Expediting the development of a structure
* Competition for resources
* Best use of personnel
* Reduction of down time
* Foreign assistance
* Getting top quality personnel into factories

In summary, there was a need for this substructure to develop maintenance and service capability. However, it too had to compete for resources. Its slow development had the consequences already described of getting 1500 organizations into the in-house hardware maintenance business. This again exacerbated the problem of competition for technically trained manpower, and led ultimately to the concept of factory service departments. (14) To supplement this and accelerate the development of a service structure, there was a push for foreign service centers coupled with cooperative and joint venture agreements. Examples are the already active Hewlitt-Packard distributorship and its service arrangements and additionally, the Perkin Elmer Service Center seen by us in Shanghai and the new Wang service center in Beijing. (54) This center co-founded by Wang Pacific Ltd. of Hong Kong and the China National Import Export Cooperative opened in Beijing January 6, 1984. MEI recognizing the continued significance for service, formed four service companies that have a dual function of service and application popularization. They are detailed in the following substructure.

The recognized problem of down time and consequent poor return on investment was being faced head on.


Application and Popularization Substructure
(See Figure 3.6)

The State Administration of the Computer Industry (SACI) was established relatively independently, but as part of the Ministry of Electronics Industry. SACI was set up to popularize the use of computers, train operators, maintenance workers, and to maintain both domestic and foreign equipment. The maintenance mission has been discussed in terms of its subsidiary, the China Computer Technical Service Corporation. SACI now known as The Administration of the Computer Industry, has offices in Beijing, Tianjin, and Shanghai; all major areas of computer concentration.

The application effort is also supported by the municipal and provincial computer center structure and emergence of user groups such as The Cooperative Society for Users of the DJS100 Series.The purpose of the user group was to :

    * exchange user experience
    * introduce the use of the DJS100 series
    * strengthen contact between users, manufacturers and design
        departments

Branches of this society have emerged in at least eight cities. Clearly, the purposes of the Cooperative Society bear on popularization.

ACI has spread the message of popularization and application recognizing application as being central to progress. Former minister of

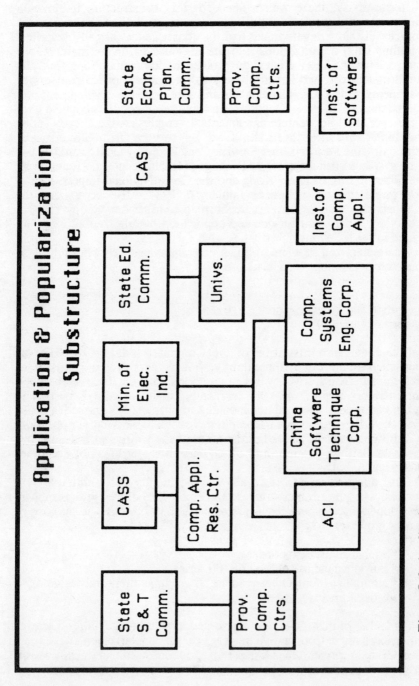

Figure 3.6 Application and Popularization Substructure

MEI, Zhang Ting, indicated in 1984 that China must emphasize micros and minis which he believed to be the key to reform of old entreprises.(175)

Popularizing application has become involved with:

* simultaneous development of medium, small and microcomputers
* developing computer systems facilities
* orienting customers and giving energetic support to technical service and developing computer literacy
* reducing cost and improving price and performance reliability of domestic computers
* accelerating building the technical bases of the computer industry
* accelerating the training of personnel and stimulating initiatives
* strengthing of foreign cooperation (67)
* development of an awareness of marketing
* solving Chinese character representation problem

Some measure of the success and scope of the application effort can be found by examining Appendix C. There is momentum behind this effort and application has gone far beyond military, engineering and scientific fields and moved towards business management, data processing and real time use in governmental departments. An important example of management use is the Computer Center of the State Planning Commission. An insight into the use of computers in drafting train charts reveals that the Harbin Railroad Bureau's computer uses predesigned mathematical models, and algorithms to quickly and accurately arrange freight routes, produce train graphs and print schedules.(17) Other current examples come from China Daily articles in 1983-84 regarding Shanghai as using over 1600 computers in banks, department stores, machine building, chemical, metallurgical, ship design, transportation, textile, and light industry and service trades. Tianjin uses 632 microcomputers for management and production in thirty five trades including public health, telecommunications and commerce.

In this substructure some of the key issues are:

* Acceleration of momentum
* Computer literacy including user friendliness
* Neutralizing automation vs. displacement
* Support of incentive systems
* Chinese character I/O

This substructure is accelerating the expanded use of computers. It has gotten into business management, movement of goods and people, productivity and efficiency. An incentive system is being implemented which is market oriented and tends to bring about coordination between developers, manufacturers, and end users. The incentive system involves multi-year contracts covering reimbursment for development, installation, orientation and training of operating personnel, maintenance and service. The multi-year contracts contain a percentage of reimbursement clauses ranging from 3% to 30%, which are based on sharing profits coming from increased productivity. (this information came from discussion with CAS personnel in the fall of 1983.) What is most interesting is that the profit sharing payback to the developer actually generates discretionary money which can be used for research equipment and wages. As a result of the 1985 MEI ACI decentralization reforms, additional emphasis was placed on bonus and penalty systems for corporations.(164)

Despite the efforts to develop computer applications, the existence of a large inventory of unused computers indicates the need for still greater efforts to continue to build a service support activity.(142) MEI and ACI recognizing this need have formed the China Software Technique Corp., the China Computer Technical Services Corp., the China Computer System Engineering Corp. and the China Computer Machine Room Engineering Corp. which are characterized as the four pillars supporting the Chinese computer industry's application and popularization efforts.(164) A measure of the encouragement of private endeavours is the emergence of the Beijing Stone Group Corp., a private computer hardware and software group that have become a leader in computer development and marketing in China.

Another initiative supporting the spread and impact of computers was reported. A Guangzhou, Shenzhen - Hong Kong microwave communications systems was opened October 7, 1983. It is intended to become part of an east-central-north China telecommunications network. It ultimately will be incorporated in the Beijing-Guangzhou coaxial cable system linking Guangzhou with Fuzhou. This new system will be able to handle 2700 simultaneous calls. Ground work is being established to upgrade telephone systems in Beijing, Shanghai and Tianjin thus adding to the momentum of these other initiatives.(62)

The China Daily also reported the actual linking of some Chinese Institutes via satellite to American and European information systems.(82) The resulting data banks will help establish the foundation for a new national information system and further increase the importance of the role of computers in China. Yang Jun, Vice Minister in charge of the State Science and Technology Committee (SSTC) listed several immediate tasks for this system including the building of modern information processing networks in large cities and industrial centers and the establishment of a bureau under the SSTC with responsibility for collection, processing and distributing scientific and technical information across China.

As a result of provincial and municipal computer centers and increased support from the expansion of training of lower level computer personnel, literacy is increasing. Literacy is also increasing as a result of exhibitions on the application of computers intending to spread the use of electronic and computer technology research results. An example was the Inner Mongolia Electronics Exhibition of Apr./May 1985.

The issue of automation versus displacement and the consequences of too much success in popularization, as yet, has not been recognized. The smaller the Chinese computer base, the more severe the problem may become. For example, a recent German study shows computerization leading to 25% fewer office jobs in public administration by 1990 in that country. The German electronics industry is too small, representing only 0.9% of the labor force for its growth to offset such projected losses. The Chinese industry will need both size and dramatic growth to offset an onrush of displacement. Given a labor intensive approach in China, the problem can become one of considerable magnitude.(69)

Education, Training and Manpower
Development Substructure (see Figure 3.7)

The Chinese Academy of Sciences, its universities, the State Education Commission's universities, the Ministry of Electronics Industry's universities all with computer programs and departments are part of this substructure. ACI's training role which is at a lower level, has already been mentioned in the section on the Application and Popularization Substructure. Complementing ACI's lower level role, secondary level computer and vocational training and technical schools have sprung up all over the country. In fact, as previously indicated, 40% of the upper middle schools will become vocational schools. The impact of joint ventures of sales contracts also come into play in building China's technically trained manpower pool. ACI's role appears here as well. For example, Li Rui reported the opening in January, 1982 of a co-sponsored SACI (now ACI), Nippon Electric Computer Software Service Center in Beijing. In addition, in the same statement, Li Rui made reference to Honeywell's agreement to train Chinese technicians (see Appendix D for various training agreements). Also reported was the October 4, 1983 opening of the Beijing Institute for Software Research and Training. This institute is a joint venture of the United Nations Financing System for Science and Technology Development, (UNFSSTD) and the Chinese government. The institute, located at the No. 2 Research School of the Beijing Polytechnic University, will enroll 30-50 graduate students at the masters level each year. Other diverse complementary efforts exist such as the Shanghai Youth Computer Technology Center, which China Daily reported as having had over 1000 students, and efforts of the Anhui Economic Commission and the Anhui Provincial Post and Telephone Office in training computer and other technical personnel to develop a computer system to provide an industrial and communications network to serve the province. In 1984 it was reported that the then Ministry of Education formed a national university software center. The center will pool work on research projects that are beyond the capacity of a single institution. It will offer technical services to government ministries, the army, industrial enterprises in management, decision making, systems analysis and simulation.(187)

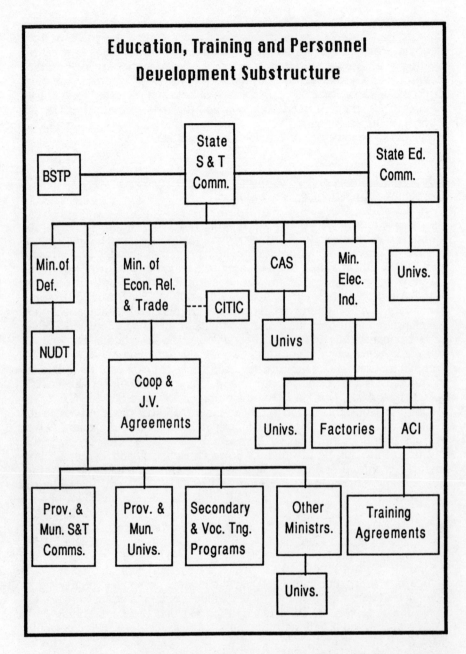

Figure 3.7 Education, Training and Personnel Substructure

Summarizing progress in technical manpower development, Li Rui reported that China's computer workforce numbered 100,000 and boasted of twenty research institutes and 86 manufacturing plants.(10) This compares reasonably with the list of factories and institutes listed in Appendix A. However, other estimates show a figure of 70,000-80,000 (70,000 alone in BNPI in 1979) workers specializing in computer research, design, manufacture, application and education. It is possible to perform a test of the accuracy of this data by examing Appendix A. If there are approximately 80 manufacturing plants and twenty developer institutes and universities with an average of 1000 employees, Li Rui's data would be fairly accurate. In 1981, SACI (now ACI) was reported as having twenty six research institutes and 99 factories. For future impact, China was reported to be planning to increase the percentage of young people participating in higher education from 5% to 13% in September, 1983. This was balanced by a statement that the absolute numbers of output of middle schools would be down.(70) Earlier in May 1983, a National Conference on Higher Education was convened. Reforms for higher education were suggested. Goals such as these were suggested:

* an annual enrollment of 550,000 in regular universities by 1987
* an increased emphasis on two to three yeaprograms to the extent that 30% of the university population would be in such programs by 1985
* a 38% increase in adult higher education
* a growth in spare time vocational and TV college population to 1.1 million by 1987

All of China's educational reforms have a potential for contributing personnel to the computer manpower pool at one level or another. The consequence of these changes and reforms, given the growth in numbers of students, computer departments and the arrival of UN and World Bank equipment, will be a plus for the training effort and ultimately trained manpower for the overall computer structure.

In 1985 a new wave of educational reforms were launched. These reforms were characterized by a continuation of patterning after US higher education and a preservation of some aspects of Soviet style education targeted on lower level technical training. The State Education Commission has replaced the Ministry of Education. An initial impact of these reforms has been the establishment at Fudan University of a School of Technological Science to coordinate teaching and research in computer science, electrical engineering, materials science and applied mechanics.(130)

As mentioned earlier, it is important to point out that other far reaching changes were proposed by Liu Dan, Honorary President of Zhejiang University and Kuang Yaming, Honorary President of Nanjing University, suggesting that the state target fifty of the more than 200 institutions of higher learning in China for top priority funding for plants, labs and libraries so that these fifty universities could graduate 500,000-600,000 baccalaureate students by 1990 and train 50,000-60,000 masters students and several thousand doctorates (elitism vs. egalitarianism comes to the fore).

At this point, in the review of the overall China computer structure, the close interrelationships, overlapping, and competition of substructures and functions should be clear. There are distinct overlaps in membership and role in R&D, education, training, manpower development, maintenance and service, and application and popularization substructures. Manpower emerges as the problem area. Clearly, it is a problem that is common to several substructures.

The capability and success of the higher education system and the support of lower level training systems in developing computer manpower are critical to the success of the entire computer structure. Central to the achievement of success in this effort is the function of the somewhat mysterious Bureau of Science and Technology Personnel (BSTP) of the Science and Technology Commission.(1)

The Chinese recognize the present and future shortage problem and are trying to work it by positive approaches related to increasing the output of a spectrum of training levels from vocational schools to graduate programs. They are also trying to increase this output by getting as much foreign training assistance as possible using the vehicle of cooperative and joint venture agreements and sending their best young minds abroad.

They may have to address in the near future the issue of limiting the size of the overall computer system in order to reduce the demand for technical manpower. However, they have recognized the problem of distribution of quality in the call to get quality computer personnel in the factory world.

Trade and Import Export Substructure
    (See Figure 3.8)

The two major ministries involved in this substructure are the Ministry of Foreign Economic Relations and Trade, and the Ministry of Electronics Industry (MEI). The Ministry of Foreign Economic Relations and Trade's major trading arm in the computer area is the National Instrument Import and Export Corporation (Instrimpex). This corporation has handled the bulk of China's computer purchases. Its #2 import department handles computers and microprocessors, including main frames, software and peripherals. The Ministry of Electronics Industry's major trading arm is the China National Electronic Technology Import/Export Corporation (CEIEC). Its 1st import department imports complete plants and technology needed in China's electronics production, while the 2nd import department imports piece products such as electronic equipment and instruments. Its 1st export department handles computers and its 2nd export department handles semi-conductor devices.

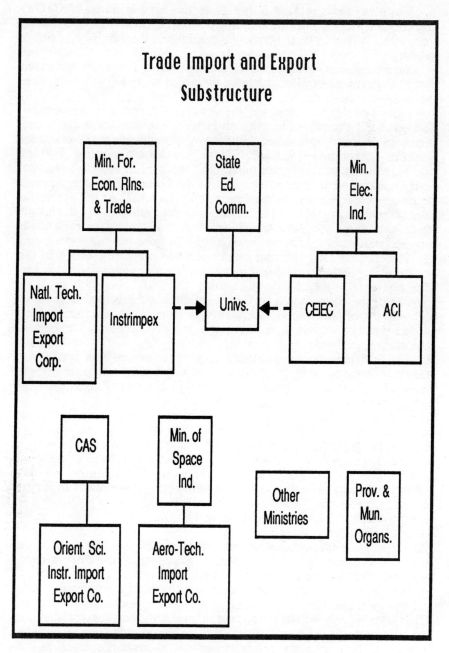

Figure 3.8 Trade Import and Export Substructure

However, the structure is not quite this simple. Each of China's former Ministries of Machine Building have established their own trading companies to handle their needs. An example is the Ministry of Space Industry's China Aero-Technology Import/Export Corp.(CATIC). Also, the Chinese Academy of Sciences formed the Oriental Scientific Instrument Import Export Corporation to handle the needs of its affiliated branches and research institutes.

Adding to this complexity is the situation that exists in the military. Relevant trading corporations and their factories can issue contracts so long as only one ministry is involved. Where several ministries are involved the New Era Corporation (Xinshidai) is the relevant organization. Foreign exchange clearance, however, must have approval of the PLA General Staff Department, the armed services or the National Defense Science Technology and Industry Commission (NDSTIC).(27) At the municipal level, as many as five steps can be involved depending on the size of the import contract. These steps could include factory, corporate, electronics and instrumentation bureaus, municipal government, and central government levels as the size of the contract increases. (169) In the meantime it appeared that CEIEC was importing for universities which had been thought to be the Instrimpex domain.

During these oscillations between centralized and decentralized control of import-export, provincial trade offices became very active establishing another substructure and overseas foreign exchange accounts. These latter were eliminated, however.

One measure of success of this portion of the overall structure, is that 500 large, medium and small computers and 10,000 micro and single board computers were imported prior to 1981 at a cost of approximately $500 million (10), with an additional expenditure of $300 million to import micros in 1984-85. By 1986 a total of 100,000 micros had been imported. Apparently, this substructure has functioned sucessfully in spite of a variety of subsurface problems such as corruption, and incompetence necessitating hand holding, payoff or bribery to expedite unloading and movement from warehouses to operational sites. Finally, there was the problem of being confronted with inadequately trained manpower to get the equipment operational.(71)

Summarizing the issues of this substructure:

* This substructure has been the major victim of oscillation between centralization and decentralization; oscillation related to changing postures on control of foreign exchange and what is imported.
* China has eliminated provincial overseas foreign exchange accounts and imposed regulations requiring hierarchical approvals if there is a request to import a computer that is available in China ; a micro that can be domestically produced; a large computer; or a computer over a certain cost level.
* In spite of the decision to centralize and tighten controls, the proliferation of import arms of governmental and other

organizations has not abated. The appearance of the new CAS Oriental Scientific Instrument Import-Export Company as well as Xinshidai are cases in point.
* Shrinking reserves of foreign currency.

The issue of accessing equipment rapidly and expediting delivery has stimulated Japanese and Southeast Asia (Hong Kong, Singapore) business and led to a resourceful use of the UN and World Bank vs. COCOM. Displeasure over this area has also led the Chinese to place penalty clauses in World Bank contracts. As already indicated, there is another side to the problem, and this is internal corruption which the Chinese are starting to cope with.

Vertical integration intrudes as an issue in a subtle way. Relative isolation of substructures does not allow the best pre-planning and coordination between policymakers, decision makers, funders, end user purchasers, shippers and operating personnel that makes certain that equipment gets into operation in the shortest possible time.

End User or Functional Substructure
    (See Figure 3.9)

Many governmental organizations and ministries have computer centers or have elements using computers. The State Planning Commission has its own computer center. The State Scientific and Technology Commission, The Ministry of Aviation Industry, The People's Bank of China, the Ministry of Commerce, and Ministry of Finance are all involved in the use of computers.(72) In 1981, The Ministry of Communications was reported considering establishing its own center while the Ministry of Geology and Minerals was reported as having three seismic processing centers in Beijing, Guangzhou, and Tianjin. The Ministry of Petroleum Industry also has three centers, the Ministry of Metallurgical Industry and the Ministry of Defense were also reported as having centers. In addition the former Ministry of Education, the Ministry of Electronics Industry, the Ministry of Foreign Economic Relations and Trade, the Ministry of Light Industry, the Ministry of Nuclear Industry, the Ministry of Ordinance, the Ministry of Post and Telecommunications and the Ministry of Public Health are all involved with computers or have centers or elements that have centers. Over twenty ministries, national governmental organizations and a broad base of industry are involved. In addition, provincial and municipal government computer centers exist and computer user associations are emerging on a national and regional basis as well as ones related to particular types of computers. The China users association held its first national conference in Guangzhou. The attendees from all over China discussed ways to accelerate the spread of computer applications and improve the relations between the computer industry and end users.

The key issues in the end user substructure link this substructure with

84

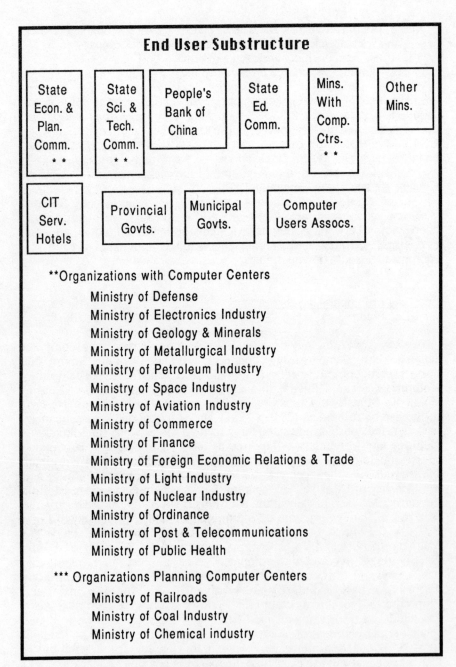

Figure 3.9  The End User Substructure

high level planning. The key issues are fundamentally, who gets what, when, and why. Decisions have to be made at a high level about priorities by functional areas including entrepreneurial initiatives and substructures. Decisions have favored ministries or organizations related to strategic considerations such as, the Defense Ministry, the Petroleum Ministry, the Ministry of Geology and Minerals; ministries involved with the rapid movement of goods and people, the undergirding of communication and consequently military command control, and defense and the development of critical natural resources.

Other issues are related to geographic placement of equipment from the points of view of dispersion and provincial/regional network approaches and optimizing options. The Chinese have certainly achieved geographic dispersion of computer centers and have been at the same time sensitive to the areas of concentration of the computer industry.

From the point of the existing and potential end user MEI has exhibited increasing sensitivity to popularization and service.


Professional Society Substucture
(See Figure 3.10)

The China Association of Science and Technology (CAST) is a comprehensive professional parent organization that cuts across the whole spectrum of S&T in China. There are now some 110 societies and associations in CAST with approximately 1000 branches representing a network and forum for interaction between all levels of S&T personnel. It is welcomed by scientists and government alike.(1) Howard Klien (51) quotes from Zhou Peiyuan's remarks at the second STA Congress in 1980; "The phenomena of looking down on knowledge and discriminating against intellectuals still exists to a fairly large extent and the role of scientists and technicians has not yet been brought into full play." The 12th Party Congress in the early fall of 1982 tried to reassure the academicians, intellectuals, and scientists that they recognized the seriousness of the problem Zhou had identified.

The various societies and groups that relate to the computer area directly or indirectly are:

* The Computer Society (28 local branches and 10,000 members) (153)
* China Microcomputer Society
* The Chinese Computer Language Society
* The Automation Society
* The Communication Society
* The Electronics Society
      The Shanghai Electronics Society-microcomputer group
* The Electrical Engineering Society
* The Association for Standardization

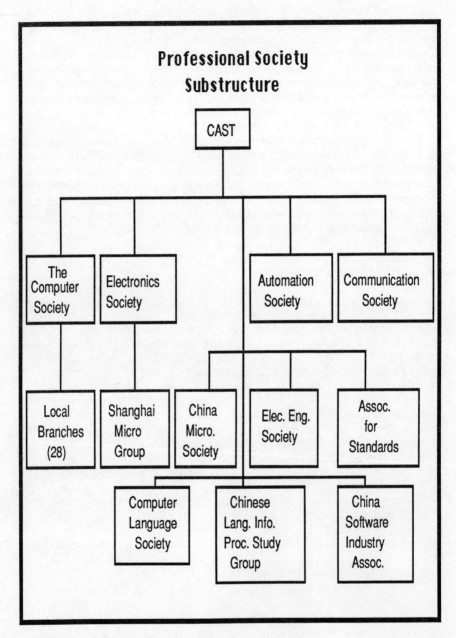

Figure 3.10 Professional Society Substructure

* The Chinese Language Information Processing Study Group
* China Software Industry Association

The professional society substructure issues essentially are professional/political issues. They involve stability, security, status for intellectuals, optimizing their utilization to bring the full weight of science to bear, improving professional competency and standards and helping to define China's desired status in the computer world.

The reactions against "the leftist tendencies" and the actions of the 1982 party congress reflect considerable sensitivity to stability, security, and status and concern over optimizing the contribution of this substructure. This concern was reemphasized by the student demonstrations in late 1986 and attempts were made to allay the fears of the professionals, with the State Council hastening to indicate that scientific, technical professional discussion was still not only acceptable but was encouraged.

Concern over standards is being evidenced in a variety of ways including participation in international meetings and in the formation of a high level computer standards group.

CAST also participated in a 1983 meeting called by the Technical Economic Research Center which is under the State Council. Ma Hong, Director of the Economic Center, said the project would draw together scientists and experts from CAS, CASS, and CAST and institutes connected with Chinese ministries, commissions, and universities to make projections for China's science and technology, employment and population, defining goals for 1985, 1990 and 2000.

Military Substructure (See Figure 3.11)

The major components of the military computer substructure are:

*The National Defense S&T and Industry Commission (NDSTIC) (CITIC link)
* The National University of Defense Technology
* The National University of Defense Technology's computer factories.
* The Fourth Bureau (NDSTIC) handles electronics and probably is the link to the Ministry of Electronics Industry
* The Academy of Military Sciences
* The People's Liberation Army
* The General Logistics Department
* The General Logistics Department's computer center

The seven bureaus of NDSTIC are: civilian use machinery and appliances, atomic energy, aircraft, electronics, weapons, ships, and missles. It is through these bureaus that contact is made with the now

88

redesignated former Ministries of Machine Building. In the context of this report, for example, the Fourth Ministry of Machine Building is now the Ministry of Electronic Industry.

The top research and development organ of the military is also the NDSTIC. Its functions are:

* to plan all military research and development activities and supervise their implementation,
* to allocate R&D funds and scrutinize their use
* to issue instructions to S&T related organizations of the industrial, academic and military sectors,
* to plan and guide science and technology related education at various service academies (74)

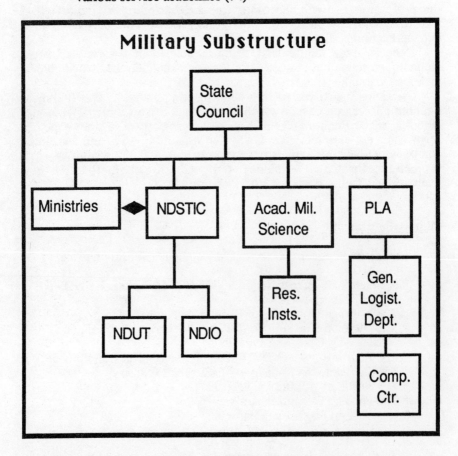

Figure 3.11 Military Substructure Relating to Computers

The breadth of these functions certainly makes it possible for the military to have a great impact on the development of computers from the point of view of design criteria, performance capabilities, and production priorities. Szuprowicz cited a Reichers estimate that in 1972 "at least half the computers operating in China were in military oriented industrial research applications."(34) While this percentage may have diminished somewhat, in the 1980s, because of the growing number and more and more varied applications of computers in China, the percentage undoubtedly remains very high when viewed in a strategic military sense such as, the ability to wage war, to handle air traffic control, computerization of transportation control, containerization of ports, and exploration and development of natural resources. Thus, there is in fact evidence today of a significant impact of the military on the computer world. A succinct statement of their approach is: "The main requirements affecting computer hardware configurations are speed, capability of simultaneous operation, reliability and cost". (75)

It is possible to comment in more specific terms on the use of computers and the thinking about the use of computers by the military and its achievements in the computer area. The National University of Defense Technology was previously known as the Harbin Military Engineering College. In 1970, it moved to Changsha and in 1978 it became the National Defense Science and Technology University. The Changsha Institute of Technology is a part of the university. The institute has a fully equipped experimental factory. The university faculty totals about 1500 teachers and professionals with 210 ranking higher than Assistant Professors.(76) A graduate school with programs leading to the Master and Ph.D. are available at the university.

This university has a Department of Electronic Computers with facilities that included a Honeywell DPS6 with 30 remote terminals and approximately 40 IBM PC's all being used in the educational process. They plan to obtain a NEC 8600 capable of 5 mops with storage of 32 mbytes. A fully equipped modern factory capable of building computers and a service factory were also part of the department. The department has lecture rooms and research offices designed for both software and hardware studies. As a result of its research projects, this department has developed 13 different types of computers, one of these was a central computer used on board a data collection ship during a rocket test firing in the Pacific.(76) Its latest achievements are the Galaxys the origonal of which is reported as capable of 100 million ops. It is an advanced fourth generation computer, and adjunct equipment available includes a preprocessor and a digital bionic simulator.

The automation, computer circuit, memory, software research and three stage control plus computer methods and quality control groups labs were all involved in the development of the Galaxys.(130)

It is also possible to report on the existence and function of the PLA Computer Center which services the General Logistics Department. It went into operation in May 1981, and serves all sections of the General

Logistics Department such as armament, financial affairs, public health, fuel supplies, and units in Beijing. It also is involved in such special projects as general survey of army radar equipment, army auto parts stock, statistics on the Army's logistic strength and accounts for national defense expenditures.(77) The ability to computerize general logistical planning, estimates of types and quantities of weapons to be produced, and where and when they are to be distributed is a substantial step forward The importance of logistic support is emphasized in the late 1982 statement of Defense Minister Zhang Aiping: "As our national economy develops, the main characteristics of our army's modern weapons and equipment are automation, high speed, flexibility and complexity resulting from a high degree of mechanization and computerization. This sets ever more arduous and complicated tasks in insuring logistic support."(167)

Military thinking about computer development and use is revealed in an article entitled Systems Engineering for Military Command Control, which states "All new computer technologies have been utilized to assure that response time for the commanders' information requests will be less than three seconds. If this requirement cannot be met, perceptual effectiveness will be decreased . At present, the weak link is input/output equipment...." In conclusion, it was pointed out that hardware and software must be effectively coordinated so that the commander can carry out his command functions by using ordinary language in direct operation of the computer.(75) The continuing improvement in Chinese character I/O will have important significance in this regard. In 1985 it was reported that commanders used Chinese character terminals in directing division commanders in an antiairborne exercise. As early as 1984 there were reports of computers being used in command and guidance systems for fighter aircraft. Also results of calculations for artillery firing has been improved by using a computer to reduce the time required. (155) Complementing these kinds of developments is the test manufacturing of the ruggedized model of the 1155-1 a high grade computing system for use under adverse conditions. (156) Some PLA units have used computers in military training, administrative work and logistics. The Fuzhou military region using micros was able to select and carry out the best offensive battle plan at divisional and regimental levels including the development of logistic supply plans for personnel, fuel, ammunition and other equipment .(180)

Both the ability to computerize, to provide statistical information and to do it in an acceptable time frame for military conditions requires highly sophisticated computer sources. At least two factors must be considered; speed of computing is imperative so that replies may be obtained in acceptable time, and internal accessible storage of large magnitude must be available so that recall can be quickly obtained. Machines having at least 10 million words of core storage and speeds of at least 10 million instructions per second, would be needed in order to have the necessary minimal capability. With the Galaxy machines, probably some of these requirements are met.

The question of what the role of computers might be in overall broad military planning in China should alsobe examined. For example, the proper size computer (large enough) might be used to calculate the optimum rate of military modernization. In an article covering the change in US policy on the sale of military support equipment to China, this thinking was suggested in a report of six economists who were drawing up a proposal for compiling the first national input/output tables in 1981.(78)

A sample of some computer achievements of the military and military related ministries and organizations are:

* A giant hydraulic press controlled by a  digital computer was developed to build guided missles (79)
* An automated test bed of relatively high  precision was developed for aircraft engine testing (80)
* An artificial satellite laser range finder  linked to a computer achieving complete automation of the observation process  has been developed and installed in Shanghai, Beijing, Kunming, Zhengzhou, Xian and Guangzhou. Based on  forecast of the satellite flight orbit, the computer  directs the telescope to focus on the target, once the telescope has tracked the satellite, the computer then  commands the transmission of laser pulses (81)
* Japanese space researchers reported that  China's newly developed CSSX4 rockets  could reach the US and drop atomic bombs hundreds of times more powerful than the  one that demolished Hiroshima. This rocket can easily be  converted into an ICBM with an effective range of 6300  miles. It can carry three megatons of  warheads. The estimated operational date was 1985. Significant for this report,  China was simultaneously reported as developing advanced control apparatus. This probably involves computers.(83)
* China also sucessfully launched 11 artificial satellites between 1970 and 1981. Tracking stations were established  in Weinan, Xian, Changchun, Kunming, and Naning. At the launching ground at Shuang-Chengzi, there are two DJS19's and at Weinan there are two DJS19's and two TQ15A's.(84) All of these computers are small.
* Luda class destroyers were used in the South Pacific ICBM testing in 1980. They were accompanied by two satellite tracking ships and two ocean observation  ships. Some of these ships were equipped with computers. Over 20 large, medium and small sized computers capable of one to several million ops were involved.(85,86) The Luda destroyers and the new class of Jianghu frigates lack combat information centers but there are plans to create space for such  centers during overhauls.
* In October, 1982  China launched a submarine based carrier rocket to a designated area in the Pacific. This was facilitated by

new developments in China's carrier rocket technology which evolved subsequent to the May, 1980, Pacific launch. Chinese made precision instruments controlled by computers transmitted information from air, land and survey ships. Thousands of in-flight data were obtained. (87,88) In 1984 it was reported that the Chinese have two Han Class submarines that have test fired cruise missles. This involves continued application of computers.(182)

* During the First National Conference on Clinical Application of Computer Software held in Nanjing in 1980, the Nanjing Command General Hospital demonstrated the multipurpose mini system DJS131. At this same meeting,China's first cooperative network for computerized medical use software wasset up with 38 units participating. Since the Nanjing Command General Hospital hosted the conference, it can be concluded that they either participated in the network exercise or learned how to establish a network.(6)

*The CAS Institute of Computer Technology's 757, 10 million ops vector computer.

* The Galaxy, capable of 100 million ops with its preprocessor and simulator.

* The YIDOYU-1, an application software development of the Chinese Aeronautical Research Institute, designed to perform optimal calculations for large structures including airplane wings under multiple constraint conditions. It took approximately three years of development work on the Ximengzi 7760 computer.(89)

* The development of a new coding program that allows a computer technician to use a 26 key keyboard to call up 7000 Chinese characters. The system is based on five strokes and four basic shapes that can attain speeds of 100 characters per minute. (90)

Undergirding this substructure is budget. A comment made to us during our September 1982 field trip, relating to the military R&D budget is in order at this point. A spokesman at Qinghua University reported that the military budget dwarfed the R&D budgets available to the Academy of Sciences and the Academy of Social Sciences.

However, the relative ranking or competitive status of the military R&D budget may be shifting somewhat in the context of the four modernizations. Robert Salter reported in May 1981, that "China's current economic program certainly calls for a cut in the defense budget and it promises to give defense modernization the lowest priority among the four modernizations." (91) In contrast, Lt. Gen. James A. Williams, Director of the US Defense Intelligence Agency, indicated that after a 13% drop in 1981, "the military share of China's budget for 1982 increased 6% compared to a 4% increase in the central government budget." Williams went on to suggest that Beijing was placing slightly more emphasis on military programs with some hidden funding. Finally, Williams indicated that nine defense related former Ministries of Machine Building are slated to achieve a 43% production increase in the next five year plan. This is particularly interesting in that Li Rui (SACI) in October 1982, was talking about a 62% increase in large, medium, and small computers during January to August of 1982 as contrasted to January to August of 1981.(10)

Supporting William's point of view about hidden funding it was reported by a different source that only about one half of the total military expenditures appear in the publicly announced figures. (137) In contrast to zealous security efforts of the Academy of Military Science which precludes interaction between its research institutes and research institutes of the CAS, other parts of the military substructure are reaching out. A change in US policy reflected in former Secretary of Defense Brown's announcement that the US was prepared to sell China items such as radar, and communications equipment have led to approval of specific export applications for tactical air defense radar sets, jet engine test devices, tropospheric communications, early warning radar antennas and passive counter measures such as chaff. In addition, the British have obtained a contract to install Seacat SAM, the HELO facility and modern CIC equipment on Luda and Kiangnan class ships.(92)

The outreach has achieved some aggressive characteristics. Lt. Gen. Williams also testified that " ploys such as the establishment of bogus trade companies, the use of friendly countries as third parties, misrepresentation of end use and the use of Chinese delegates and exchange students to obtain desired items were employed to bolster legitimate trade methods of obtaining technology needed for the military modernization program."(93) Others have become involved. FBI agent James Nealis was cited as noting in a Philadelphia Inquirer article of March 22, 1984 that five people in Newark, NJ were allegedly trying to smuggle computers to China.

There is probably ample data in the Southeast Asia computer market and in particular, in Hong Kong to indicate that Chinese controlled companies are expediting access to computer equipment that could not come directly to China, and that they are getting the opportunity to have equipment and consequently examine technology. A case in point is the IBM equipment at the Bank of China in Hong Kong.

This tends to support another of William's points. The Chinese are using such channels because of impatience with US export controls. Hard evidence of Chinese displeasure over these controls in the computer market is found in their stance in the World Bank bidding.The China National Technical Import Corporation, the procurement agent for the project, insisted that regardless of export license delays, the delivery schedule must be met or else they would require a penalty of 0.5% for each week behind scheduled delivery up to ten weeks. If delivery is more than ten weeks late, the supplier may have its contract forfeited and give up its 15% performance bond at the option of the Chinese buyer. (12) Exacerbating this attitude of the Chinese and their feeling of frustration over export control, is the fact that while the Reagan Administration has even gone beyond the Carter Administration in removing China from the list of prohibited destinations for purposes of the Munitions Control List, Carter and Reagan policies have been effectively thwarted at the working level.(94) In 1985 COCOM agreed to relax export restrictions to the PRC on 27 categories including computers and components.(138)

In reaching out, other problems have arisen. Salter reports that China had difficulty in using the relatively sophisticated airplane engine technology of the Soviet MIG21 and the Rolls Royce Spey engine. He saw this as being symptomatic of a broader China technical weakness severely enforced by the disruptive impact of the cultural revolution on higher education.(91) Except for a small cadre, this technical weakness exists in understanding the cutting edge of the computer world.

Key computer issues of the military substructure involve:

* Budget allocation, competition with CAS, the former Ministry of
    Education, and the Ministry of Electronics Industry, for
    computers, R&D computer monies and operating money
*Division of money between basic and applied research
* How much influence shall the military have on design criteria such
    as speed, simultaneous calculation, reliability, minaturization,
    portability? Is the military the driving force behind the extensive
    effort and the substantial allocation of resources to solve the
    problem of Chinese character representation? Is this for the
    purpose of simplifying and speeding up command control input
    and output on computers?
* Networking
* Geographic distribution of computers and centers
* Expeditious movement of aircraft, ships supplies and personnel
* Energy conservation
* Development of strategic natural resources
* How best to close the computer gap between China and the
    external computer world.
*The decision making process that controls what computer
    information can be transferred to the civilian sector.

Everything from the outstanding comprehensive computer effort at the National University of Defense Technology's computer center to the existence of a PLA computer center serving the General Logistics Department to the fact that computers capable of one and two million ops were involved in the 1980 ICBM testing, indicate that the military is well funded and gets quality equipment.

While there is no available data indicating the division of monies between basic and applied computer research, one can speculate that because defense is a mission oriented effort, emphasis is placed on applied and developmental work. The consequence of this is that in competition, basic computer research which has a non preferred status probably suffers in obtaining an appropriate percentage of available funds. The generally preferred budget status of the military may have still another effect on research. To the degree that university research cadres are entrepreneurial, and pursue funds outside their own budgets, the military may lead them into an applied emphasis. To the degree that all of this is true, and change may be in the making, it will become more and more difficult to pursue the cutting edge.

The cutting edge these days includes Very Large Integrated Circuits (VLICs) and Very High Speed Integrated Circuits (VHSICs), which is the pursuit of a faster and faster chip. This becomes critical for the military because each new generation of electronic weaponry is dependent on ever faster and more complex controls. This type of research to date has been beyond Chinese capability. They have been struggling with VLICs not VHSICs and their chip yield has been poor. Therefore, there has been a compounding of the problem between the applied emphasis and the lack of cutting edge capability.

Certainly, the military objectives of geographic dispersion of computer centers and prioritized allocation of computers to ministries connected with strategic roles have been carried out reflecting a major impact. In the context of even broader defense strategic considerations and command control, the military is expected to develop alliances with the Academy of Science, academia, and ministries to push networking and implement a major upgrading of the communication system. To date, we have no evidence of their direct involvement in expediting achievement of goals in computer networking in the five year plans for Xian and Shanghai. However, there is evidence of microwave and coaxial cable upgrading and utilization of a cooperative network for computerized medical software.

In conclusion, the military has to face the same constraints in computer achievements as the civilian sector.

* China has to remain politically stable to be able to systematically carry out research and assimilate foreign computer technology.
* China has a growing need for highly trained technical manpower.
* China has to access as much advanced foreign computer technology and equipment as possible.

In the context of improved defense technology and equipment base, John R. Sloan of the US Defense Intelligence Agency has said: " China's only hope for significant improvement is through acquisition of foreign systems by purchase and co-production."(95) This, while it is a general statement, might have been true for the military computer world in China. However, there appear to be hidden and significant capabilities and advanced equipment which we and others had not seen which dramatically lead the civilian sector.

## IV. CONCLUSION

Fang Yi, at the National Science Conference of 1978 in setting forth the comprehensive 1978-85 Science and Technology Plan had this to say about computers: "China must make a big new advance in computer science and technology. We should lose no time in solving the science and technology problems in the production of large scale integrated circuits, and make a breakthrough in the technology of ultra large scale integrated circuits. We should study and turn out a giant computer, put a whole range of computers in serial production, step up study on peripheral equipment, on software for computers and on applied mathematics and energetically extend the application of computers. We aim to acquire, by 1985, a comparatively advanced force in research in computer science and build a fair size, modern computer industry. Microcomputers will be popularized and a giant ultra high speed computer put into operation. We will also establish a number of computer networks and data bases. A number of key enterprises will use computers to contol the major processes of production and management." (39)

In the spring of 1983, Fang Yi expanded in more detail to the State Council's Leading Group for the Invigoration of the Electronics Industry as follows

* China's modernization is impossible without technology.
* Research work should be focused on medium size computers, small computers, and microcomputers, for a considerable period of time.
* A software industry should be established in the quickest time possible
* Efforts should be concentrated on production of medium and small scale integrated circuits in the coming three to five years
* International exchange, cooperation, and trade contacts should be strengthened and expanded. The know-how, materials, equipment and spare parts which are urgently needed and not available in China should be imported directly or through co-production and

97

technical patent information
* China must build its own computer system by the 1990's (35)

In 1983 China Letter evaluated China's computer industry development as being far behind that of advanced countries. Our diagnosis is that the China computer world's major problems relate to :

* Manpower: demand and supply, quality of manpower, allocation of manpower, training of manpower, incentives for improving performance of manpower, and optimizing the use of manpower
* Manufacture: implementation of national computer standards, serialization and mass production , acquisition of precision machinery, acquisition of high speed precision machinery, and development of a cadre of precision machine personnel
* Management: an inadequate infra-structure, insufficient numbers of properly trained managers, and the need for much more emphasis on management training and skill in the decision making process
* Resource allocation decisions: in terms of money, research equipment and location of powerful computers, personnel, and networks, location of modern phone systems, dedicated lines , micro-wave stations, and satellites, and access to all of them.

In evaluation of achievement of the ambitious set of goals of 1978 and their subsequent modification, China has done reasonably well considering where it started in 1978. While achievement has been both significant and uneven, the degree of priority has been uncertain in an experimental transition period. Given lack of experience, the second and third order of conseqence of courses of action may not have been thought through. This temporarily resulted in unplanned overemphasis on hardware at the expense of peripherals and software, hardware essentially divorced from software, processors divorced from systems, and mainframes divorced from application. On the positive side, there has been a lessening in the degree of divorce, an increasing focus on both software and solution of the pervasive Chinese character representation problem. Also there is a mitigation of the strict adherance to vertical integration. In pursuit of a middle course China is both importing computers and computer parts while at the same time trying to develop its own production. In 1985 Zhang Aiping, Minister of the Ministry of Defense and Deputy Secretary General of the Communist Party Central Committee's Military Commission called on the computer industry to strive for independence and self reliance, improving quality and increasing competitivnes. However, he recognized that while domestic products were being developed, China would still have to import key electronic parts.(162) To support this point Vice Premier Li Peng in January 1986 supported developing a domestic computer industry by calling for the utilization of domestically made components. (145) Significant and uneven achievement has left China behind the computer universe, even further behind in 1986 than in 1978, because of the rate of progress achieved in the external computer universe in megachips, super chips, and Japanese and US efforts to achieve fifth generation computers by 1990 that will include parallel processing and will be capable of 10 billion ops or more. The Chinese in developing their new machines are well aware of the advantages and problems associated with parallel processing. The Chinese expressed interest as early as 1984 in acquiring the best advanced large computer manufactured either at home or abroad and capable of more than 100 million calculations per second. The machine is expected to be used to supply accurate weather forecasts from 7 to 10 days in advance. A spokesman for the Central Meteorological Bureau stated that China expects to put such a computer into operation around 1990.(176) It appears that the Chinese will find it difficult to import a computer having a capability of Cray machines unless in the unlikely event that by 1990 significant changes in US or Japanese computer technology make these machines outdated. Therefore the Chinese will be forced to rely on their own resources to produce a more powerful machine than they have been able to produce to date. In consideration of the technology that exists in China in 1986 and the technology they can import, the probability of their producing a machine having a speed considerably more than 100 mops is small.

We believe that China, in spite of positive statements regarding their achievements, recognized by 1982 what the real situation was and decided on a long term approach of :

* A continued high military priority for computers
* A limited general priority for computers. Only in 1982 was computer science added to the National Science Foundation (NSF) and Chinese Academy of Sciences (CAS) protocols.
* An outreach through the United Nations and World Bank for computer acquisition
* Developing an open door policy focusing on joint ventures, specific trade and economic zones, tax breaks, training support, technology acquisition, technology transfer, and ultimately exportable products
* Building of substantial foreign exchnge reserves as a strong creditor nation to facilitate importation of computers

Basically, this approach is one that reflects a temporary shift from doing it entirely on your own to doing some on your own and acquiring as much as can be acquired from outside given the special barrier of COCOM regulations (A classic case is the fast track development of the Galaxy). This approach also reflects a belief that time will allow China to solve most of the manpower and resource allocation related problems. The machining-equipment problem is more serious and won't be solved with the passage of time and will continue to exist as an outcome of the COCOM barrier.

This interim policy may put China, by the year 2000, in a position where they can start to close the gap between themselves and the external computer universe. We certainly agree with the interim Chinese policy and evaluation of John R. Sloan that "China's only hope for significant improvement is through acquisition of foreign systems by purchase and co-production" .(95)

China had a serious computer setback as a result of the impact of the Cultural Revolution, but the passage of time will eliminate its negative impacts. Much of Chinese computer achievement and optimism and planning up until this time has tended to completely underestimate the rate of progress that the external computer universe could achieve. The bottom line is that China will not be in a position to stabilize the gap, let alone close the gap, between itself and the external computer universe at least until the year 2000. In a longer term view, China has not begun to address the problem of job elimination resulting from wide spread computer application and what that may do to the still unsettled future of the intellectual in China.

The current Chinese computer policy is driven by the geopolitical reality of the presence of the Soviet Union on the long exposed Chinese frontier and a powerful nationalistic undercurrent. Such a policy has not foreclosed the option of developing in a competitive way a software export effort. It is much easier to compete in the software marketplace if one is developing software for one's own machines than to compete with another country's computer manufacturers in developing software for their products.

In evaluating the data in Figure 4.1, Generation Comparison of Main Frames, and Appendix F, Gap Estimates, and additional comparative data it becomes clear that the major players in the computer world in rank order are the US, Japan, USSR, Western European countries and China. What we have indicated is that possibly by the year 2000 the Chinese may challenge Western Europe and the USSR in competitive rank. Clearly, such countries as India and Brazil are not currently competitive and will not become so. India by emphasizing the external purchase of hardware and the internal development of software has removed itself from the arena of hardware competition and basically foreclosed the option of competing successfully in software development. It is in the software field in a very disadvantageous posture. Brazil in contrast, a debt burdened nation, in attempting to develop a computer industry has neither forclosed its software development option nor put itself at a serious competitive disadvantage in the development of software. However, because of lack of investment capital, the hardware developed will probably be limited to micro or PC production. Even there it will probably not make significant progress unless expert foreign technology is brought in via the joint venture approach used in China.

## GENERATION COMPARISON OF MAIN FRAMES

| | China | ops | USSR | ops | USA | ops |
|---|---|---|---|---|---|---|
| First generation Vacuum tube | 1. August 1<br>2. DJS1<br>3. DJS2<br>(1958–63) | 2K<br>1.8K<br>10K | Ural 1<br>(1951) | 12K | IBM 701<br>(1947–51) | 20K |
| Second generation transistors | 1. DJS6<br>(1966–67)<br>2. 109C | 100K<br>115K | 1. M20<br>(1959–60)<br>2. BSEM 6 | 50K<br>1M | | 120K<br>850K |
| Third generation IC's | 1. 111<br>(1970–82)<br>2. DJS11<br>3. 013<br>4. HDS9 | 100K<br>1M<br>2M<br>5M | 1. NAIRI 3<br>(1968–73)<br>2. RIAD 1060<br>3. BESEM<br>(1980) | 1.5M<br>1.5M<br>10.6M | 1. CEC 7600<br>(1969–74)<br>2. Illiac IV | 11+M<br>100M |
| Fourth generation | 1. 757<br>2. Galaxy | 10M<br>100M | | | 1. Cray 1<br>2 Cyber 205 | 200M<br>200M |

Fig. 4.1  Generation Comparison of Main Frames

# V. REFERENCES

1. Orleans, L. A., Report, Committee on Scholarly Communication with the People's Republic of China, Science Policy Study Group, National Academy of Sciences, 1/82, pp 27, 33-34."Some Issues and Observations."
2. Smith, J. K. L., and Witzell, O. W., Unpublished transcript of tapes of 1982 visit.
3. China Report, JPRS 81620, Science and Technology # 171, 8/24/82, p. 20.
4. Daily Report, China, FBIS-CHI-83010, 1/14/83, p.K13.
5. China Report, JPRS 78669, Science and Technology #115, 8/14/81, p. 21.
6. China Report, JPRS 75797, Science and Technology # 38, 5/30/80, p. 91.
7. China Report, JPRS 80282, Science and Technology # 152, 3/10/82, p. 23.
8. Daily Report, China, FBIS-CHI-82168, 8/30/82, p. B1.
9. Daily Report, China, FBIS-CHI-82033, 2/18/82, p. E2.
10. Daily Report, China, PRC National Affairs, FBIS- CHI-82205, 10/22/82, p. K16-17.
11. Jiachon Peng, China's Growing Computer Industry, China Reconstructs, 2/82, p. 33.
12. Brown, C., Computer Sales, China Business Review, March/April 83, pp. 30-32.
13. China Computerworld, 9/20/82, p 16; 12/20/82, p 16; 1/20/83 p16.
14. US Government Trade Analysts, The Benefits of Financial Conservativism, China Business Review, Jan/Feb 83, pp. 48-49.
15. Daily Report, China, FBIS-CHI-82149, 8/30/82,p. G3.
16. Daily Report, China, FBIS-CHI-82162, 8/20/82,p. K21.
17. China Report, JPRS 82980, Science and Technology #189, Computer Development and Application II, March, 1, 1983, pp. 9, 16.

18. Jammes, S. H., Implications of US China Military Cooperation, Committee on Foreign Relations, US Senate, Congressional Research Service, Library of Congress, 1/82, p. 24.
19. Various Chinese and Japanese Publications.
20. Little, Jennifer, Exports to China, China Business Review, Mar./ Apr. , 83.
21. China Report, JPRS 81896, Science and Technology #175, 9/30/82, p. 13.
22. China Daily, Vol. 2, # 479, 9, Feb., 1983.
23. Auerbach, Computing in China, April/May 1979.
24. Sherman, H., Electrotechnology in China, Perspective, 1978.
25. China Report, JPRS 74826, 12/27/79, p 29.
26. China Computerworld #21, p. 13.
27. Sullivan Roger W., US Military Sales to China, The China Business Review, Mar/Apr 1986, p. 8.
28. China Computerworld, 2/20/83, p. 15.
29. Daily Report, China, FBIS-CHI-80178, 9/11/80, p.L21.
30. Grey, Aeronautics in China, Chap. XI.
31. Garner, H. L., Computing in China, March, 1979.
32. Sigurdson, J., Note on China's Computer Industry, Aug., 23, 1983.
33. China Daily, Computers to Improve Production Management, Vol. 3, # 752, 12/22/83.
34. Szuprowicz, B., Electronics in China, 7/78, Chap. 21, pp. 46-47, 52.
35. Xinhua, 5/16/1983.
36. Holland, W. B., Perspectives on Chinese Computing, Soviet Cybernetics Review, Jan., 73, p. 20.
37. Daily Report, China, FBIS, CHI-80118, PRC National Affairs, 6/17/80, p.L5.
38. Clark, C. M., Dewenter, K. L., China Business Manual, 1981, National Council on US China Trade, Washington D. C., pp. 130, 142.
39. Orleans, L. A., Science in Contemporary China, Appendix A, 3/18/78, pp. 547-551.
40. Graham, M., Principal Laws Governing Foreign Investments in China, China Business Review, Sept./Oct. 1982.
41. Suttmeier, R. P., US/PRC Scientific Cooperation: An Assessment of the First Two Years, US State Department Study, 6/81, pp. 2 and 62-65.
42. Sterling, J. M. D., Mystery of Two Honeywells, Asian Computer Monthly, July, 1980.
43. China Market, China Adopts New Measures to Develop IC and Computer Technology, September, 1983, pp. 66-67.
44. Aeronautical Knowledge, The Amazing Silicon Chip, 5/79, pp. 25-27.

45. Beijing Review, Americans Talk about Sino US Relations, Vol. 27, #1, Jan. 2, 1984.
46. Smith, J. K. L., and Lee, J. L., Private Discussions. 1982.
47. Terry, E., Decentralizing Foreign Trade in Fujian Province, China Business Review, September/October, 1980, pp. 11-19.
48. Bradshaw, D., Language Problems Slow China Computer Process, Art Processing, Feb. 1982, p. 11.
49. Zhonguo, Kexue, Jishu Qingbao Yangiuso Jianjie, 1978, (ISTIC).
50. Szuprowicz, B., Computer Data, 4/79.
51. Asian Computer Monthly, (end user article), 10/79.
52. Daily Report, China, FBIS-CHI-82246, 12/22/82, p.K28.
53. Daily Report, China, FBIS-CHI-82164, 8/24/82, p. K19.
54. China Computerworld, 3/20/83, pp. 16, 17.
55. China Report, JPRS Summary, China Examines Science Policy 80-82, Computer Application Popularization Making Rapid Progress. 1/82, pp.184,190,191.
56. China Market Intelligence, US Firm Wins in Main Frame Bidding 12/82, p.157. Electronic Buyer's News, China to Allow Foreign Firms, Manhasset, NY, 7/2/79, pp. 4-6.
58. Information Systems News, Peking's New Foreign Trade Law to Spur US Information Processing Growth in PRC, N. Y., 12/10/79.
59. Peng Jian Chou, China's Growing Computer Industry, China Reconstructs, 2/82, p. 33.
60. China Report, JPRS 81249, Science and Technology, #166, 7/12/82, p.33.
61. Bulletin for Visitors, The Institute of Computing Technology, CAS, Beijing , China, Oct.,1982.
62. China Daily, Shanghai's Industry Gears to Computers, Vol. 3, No. 687, 10, Oct., 1983.
63. China Report, JPRS 82161, Science and Technology, #179, 11/4/82, p. 4.
64. China Report, JPRS 75887, Science and Technology, #40, 6/16/80, p. 63.
65. Asian Computer Monthly, China Orders 30 Australian Micros, 5/82.
66. China Electronic News, French Equipped ComputeÇompany built in Guangzhou, 5/10/82 p. 6.
67. Xu Meng Fei, Putting the Stress on Applications- Strive to Develop China's Computer Industry 9/81.
68. Simon Denis F. and Rehn Detlef, Understanding the Electronics Industry, The China Business Review Mar/Apr. 1986, pp. 10-15.
69. Botkin, J., Dimancescu, D., Stata, R., Global Stakes, Ballinger Company, Cambridge, MA, 1982, p. 28.
70. Gu, D., (VP, Chengdu Institute of Radio Eng'g.), Smith, J. K. L., Private Discussion.

71. Smith, J. K. L., Witzell, O.W., Interview with Fensterstock, J., and Birnbaum, M., Phoenix Associates.
72. China Computerworld, 9/5/82, p. 16.
73. Orleans, L. A., Science in Contemporary China, (Electronics, Szuprowicz), Stanford University Press, pp. 435-461
74. Gonji, Kenkyu, Chinese Army's Capabilities Analyzed, 7/82, pp. 42-58.
75. China Report, JPRS 80451, Science and Technology, #155, 3/31/82, pp. 26-27.
76. China Report, JPRS 81180, Science and Technology, #165, 6/30/82, p.32
77. Daily Report, China, FBIS, CHI-81232, PRC National Affairs, 12/3/81, p.K8
78. Szuprowicz, B., US Policy About Face Allows Firms to Sell China Military Support Equipment, Computer World, Framingham MA., 10/27/80.
79. Daily Report, FBIS, China, CHI-79180, PRC National Affairs, 9/14/79, p.L7.
80. Daily Report, FBIS, China, CHI-80016, PRC National Affairs, 1/23/80, p. L5.
81. China Report, JPRS 79601, Science and Technology, #139, 12/7/81 p.1.
82. China Daily, Nationwide Information Network Planned, Vol. 3, No. 778, 24, Jan., 1984.
83. Hong Kong Standard, CSSX-4 Can Hit US and Europe, (Tokyo, Nov. 12), Nov. 13, 1979, p. 6.
84. Maier, Information Technology in China, Asia Survey, Vol. XX, #8, 8/80, p. 871.
85. NY Times, China to Conduct First ICBM Testing Pacific, 5/10/80, p. 6.
86. NY Times, China Sucessfully Launches its First ICBM, 5/18/80, p. 3.
87. China Pictorial, #1, 1983, p. 3.
88. Philadelphia Inquirer Wire Service, China Tests Rocket Fired from Submarine, 10/17/82.
89. China Report, JPRS 84474, #208, 10/5/83, p 22
90. China Report, JPRS 84608, #212, 10/25/83.
91. Salter, R. G., Increased US Military Sales to China: Argument and Alternatives, 5/20/81, p. CRS11.
92. Bossert, J., Modernization of China's Military Electronics to be Slow, Defense Electronics, 10/81, pp. 73-81.
93. Washington, A. P., China Using Ploys to Gain US Technology, Patriot, Harrisburg, PA., 7/20/82.
94. Sullivan, R. W., Implications of US China Military Cooperation, Committee on Foreign Relations, US Senate and Congressional Research Service, Library of Congress, 1/82, pp. 141-142.
95 Sloan J. T., Implications of US China Military Cooperation,

Committee on Foreign Relations, US Senate and Congressional Research Service, Library of Congress, 1/82, p. 33.

96. Berney, K., China's Computer Revolution, China Business Review, Nov./Dec., 1981, p. 14.
97. Daily Report, FBIS, China PRC National Affairs, 25 Sept. 84, p. K1.
98. China Report, JPRS 75570, 4/25/80. pp. 10,16.
99. China Report, JPRS 80058, #147, 2/9/82, pp. 12, 13.
100. China Report, JPRS 80189, #150, 2/25/82. pp. 36, 38, 39.
101. China Report, JPRS 80252, #151, 3/5/82, p 19.
102. Szuprowicz, Datamation, 6/75.
103. Bowie, Electronics and Computers in China.
104. Huskey, Computing in China, Computer, Oct. ,1981, p. 42.
105 Wilhelm, N. C., Report on visit to PRC., 12/78.
106. The China Letter, #142, Aug. 1983.
107. China Report, JPRS 79805, #142, 1/6/82, pp 23, 25, 38.
108. China Report, JPRS 80143, #149 , 2/19/82, p 21.
109. China Report, JPRS 75428, #30, 4/2/80, p. 2.
110. Berney, K., China Business Review, 10/80.
111. China Report, JPRS 76149, #49, 8/1/80, p. 27.
112. China Computerworld, #5, March, 1981, p. 1.
113. China Computerworld, #17, p 127.
114. China Report JPRS 80282, #152, 3/10/82, p. 7.
115. China Computerworld, 6/5/82.
116. Asian Computer Monthly, 12/79.
117. New Scientist, 6/17/82, p.761.
118. Tao Chen, China Business Review, p. 36.
119. Asian Computer Monthly, 2/79.
120. Computer Weekly, London, 1980.
121. Computer Business News, 2/79.
122. China Business Review, 4/79 p.76.
123. Shipping and Trade News, Tokyo, 1980.
124. Asian Computer Hong Kong Monthly, Sept., 1980.
125. China Business Review, 4/80.
126. China Report, JPRS 82854, #187, 2/11/83, p. 2.
127. Wang Ju, China Adopts New Measures to Develop Integrated Circuit and Computer Technology, China Market, 9/83.
128. China Report, JPRS-CPS-84009, Political, Sociological and Military Affairs, 25, Jan., 1984.
129. China Daily, Electronics Crucial to Modernization,Vol. 3, No.671, p. 21 Sept., 1983.
130. Smith, J. K. Lee and Witzell, O.W., Tapes of 1985 & 1986 Trips.
131. Standardization Journal (Chinese) #8, 1983, The National Technical Committee of Standardization for Computer and Information Processing Estab. in Beijing, pp. 1-3.
132. Beijing Review, Galaxy Supercomputer, Vol. 27, #1, p. 21, Sept. 1983.

133. Business China, Jan. 27, 1986, p. 14.
134. Xia Chun, Subsidy to Prime Sales of Domestic Computers, China Daily , 1/22/86.
135. Beijing Has Future as Computer Capital, China Daily, 1/18/86, p. 3.
136. China Report, JPRS-CST-85013, Computer's Role in China's Industrial Advancement, 1, May, 1985, p. 10.
137. Clarke Christopher M., The Strategy and Politics of Modernizing China's Conventional Military Forces, July, 1984 p. 5.
138. COCOM opens China Trade Door Wider, The Asian Computer Monthly, Feb.1986 p.7.
139. Inside China, #16, 7, Feb. 1986.
140. Inside China, #17, 14, Feb. 1986.
141. Inside China, #44, 1, Sept. 1986.
142. Inside China, #54, 10, Nov. 1986.
143. Inside China, #28, 9, May 1986.
144. Inside China, #25, 25 Apr. 1986.
145. Inside China, #15, 31, Jan. 1986.
146. Inside China, #31, 2, June 1986.
147. Inside China, #51, 20 Oct. 1986.
148. Klein S. News Letter on Computer Graphics, 7.8 million CAD/CAED order from mainland China goes to CALMA Co., Dec. 27, 1985.
149. China Daily, Computer system to ease traffic jams,Nov. 14, 1985, p. 3.
150. Hyatt's PC News Report, Computer imports to China drop off, Oct. 1985.
151. Meilach Donna Z. Peking reverses open door policy on computer imports, PC Week, Sept. 17, 1985.
152. Wang Zhen at opening of Hewlitt-Packard venture, PRC International Affairs, US, 21 June 1985 p. B2-3.
153. China Daily, 6/12/85, p. 5.
154. China Daily, French sign computer sale deal, 5/10/85, p. 2.
155. Daily Report, FBIS, PRC National Affairs, 3, May 85, p. K7.
156. China Report, JPRS-CST-85013 , 1 May 1985, pp. 14-15, 62.
157. EDP China Report, Apr. 30, 1985 pp. 173-174, 180.
158. EDP China Report, Apr. 15, 1985 pp. 165-166.
159. China Daily, Burroughs in Business Bid, 3/16/85, p. 2.
160. Chen Liwei, China's Computer Hunt, Spectrum Supplement, Mar. 1985, pp. 3-5.
161. Australian, Honeywell Bouyant after China Sucess, Feb. 5, 1985.
162. China Daily, Computer Training, PLA Schools Open, Feb., 2, 1985, p. 3.
163. EDP China Report, Syntone Advanced Computer Technology Co.in Beijing, Feb. 1985, p. 107.
164. Ma Fuyuan, 1984 in Retrospect and 1985 in Prospect, EDP China Report, Jan 30, 1985. pp. 84-88.
165. Bangsberg P. T. China may Tighten Computer Mart, The Journal

of Commerce, Jan. 9, 1985, p. 5A.

166. Daily Report, FBIS, China, 14, Jan. 1985.

167. Daily Report, FBIS, 11/29/82.

168. China Report, JPRS-CST-85001, 1/3/85, p.16.

169. Wood H. M., Reifer D.J., Sloan M., A Tour of Computing
     Facilities in China, Computer, Jan. 1985, p. 85.

170. EDP China Report, Jan. 15, 1985 p. 71.

171. Zhenyi H., Market for Computers Opened to Foreigners, China
     Daily, Sept.6, 1984, p. 1.

172. Mitsumori K., China's Computer Trade Policy puts Japanese at
     Disadvantage, The Japan Economic Journal, Sept. 18, 1984,
     p. 4.

173. EDP China Report, Sept. 4, 1984, p. 296.

174. Computerworld, Aug. 27,1984.

175. EDP China Report, Former Minister Envisages Bright Future for
     China's Electronic Industry, Aug. 20, 1984, pp. 280, 282.

176. Zhu Ling, Weather Satellite Program on Target for Liftoff, China
     Daily, Aug. 16, 1984, p. 1.

177. Beijing Hewlitt-Packard Shape Joint Venture Firm, MIS Week,
     Aug. 15, 1984.

178. China joins the IBM PC Compatible Crowd, Electronic Business,
     Aug. 1, 1984 p. 58.

179. First Sino-Japanese Software Joint Venture opens in Japan, EDP
     China Report, July 31, 1984, p. 256.

180. Daily Report, FBIS, China PRC National Affairs, 9, July 1984,
     p. K 16-17.

181. Unclassified Telegram, US Dept. of State, 17 July 1984, p. 01.

182. Gillespie R. E., Marketing to the PLA, China Business Review,
     July/Aug. 1984, pp. 37-38.

183. Stepanek J. V., Microcomputers in China, China Business
     Review, May/June 1984, p. 27.

184. Prime Computer Deal, Australasian China Report, Apr. 1984, p. 32.

185. Manners David, Chinese Join High Tech TraiElectronics Weekly,
     London Eng., 3/21/84.

186. First Sale of US Programmers to China Completed, Defense
     Electronics, Feb. 1984, p. 27.

187. Daily Report, FBIS, China PRC National Affairs, 20, Mar.,
     1984, p. K18.

188. China Exchange News, June 1987, Vol. 15, #2, pp.27-28.

189. Private communication from Prof Victor Feng, Dept. of Physics,
     Drexel Univ. Phila. Pa.

# VI. APPENDIXES

## APPENDIX A

### Selected List of Factories, Institutes, and Universities in Manufacturing

#### Research Institutes and Universities

Beijing Area
  Beijing University Electronics  Instrument Factory
  Beijing Engineering University Factory
  Beijing Industrial University  Electronics Plant
  East China Normal University Scientific Instrument Factory
  Qinghua University Factory and Electrical Eng'g. Dept.
  North China Institute of Computing Technology (MEI)
  Research Institute of Computer Systems Engineering (MEI)
  Institute of Computing Technology (CAS)
  Institute of Software (CAS)
  Institute of Semiconductor Research (CAS)
  Beijing Broadcasting Technical Institute
  Electronic Research Application  Institute
  China Electronics Equipment  Corporations's Research Inst. of
     Communication

Fujian Province
  Fujian Electronic Technology Institute

Guangdong Province
  Huanan Shifan University Factory

Heilongjiang Province
  Harbin Industrial University

111

Harbin Research Institute of Electronic Components
Harbin Longkou Institute
Heilongjiang Electric Institute

Hubei Province
Hubei Computer Technology Research Institute

Hunan Province
Changsha Research Inst. of Equipment for Semiconductor
Technology
National University of Defense Technology (Changsha Inst. of
Technology)

Jiangsu Province
Yangzhou Automation Research Institute
Nanjing Aeronautic Institute
Nanjing University
Suzhou Electronics Technology Research Institute

Liaoning Province
Shenyang Research Institute
Institute 1447 (Shenyang)

Shaanxi Province
Shaanxi Electronics Institute

Shanghai Area
Fudan University
Jiaotung University
Huadong Normal University
Huadong Computing Technical Institute
East China Institute of Computer Technology (MEI)
Shanghai Teachers University
Shanghai Institute of Computing Technology
Shanghai Computational Institute
Shanghai Metallurgical Institute (CAS)
Shanghai Municipal Mech. and Elec. Products Design Institute

Tianjin Area
Tianjin Radio Technical Institute
Tianjin Magnetic Recording Technical Research Institute

Zhejiang Province
Wenzhou Electronics Technology Research Institute

Numbered Institutes
#6 Institute

# 15 Institute
# 1421 Institute
# 1915 Institute
# 1932 Institute

Factories

Anhui Province
  Anhui Radio Factory

Beijing Factories
  Beijing #1 Computer Factory
  Beijing #2 Computer Factory
  Beiing #3 Computer Factory
  Beijing #4 Computer Factory
  Beijing #5 Computer Component Factory
  Beijing Electronics Factory (MEI)
  Beijing #1 Peripheral Equipment Factory
  Beijing #2 Peripheral Equipment Factory
  Beijing Dongguang Electronics Factory
  Beijing Changceng Machine Factory
  Beijing China Computer Technical  Service Corp.
  Beijing Lishan Micro Electronic Corp.
  Beijing Wire Communication Factory
  Beijing Lienhu Radio Plant

Fujian Province
  Fujian Broadcating Equipment Factory
  Xiamen Computer Factory
  Gutain Dianssheng Equipment Factory
  Fuzhou Radio Factory

Guangdong Province
  Shenzui Electronic Assembly Plant
  Jiangmen #2 Radio Factory
  Guangdong Nanhai Radio Plant
  Yuan Hua Electrical Co.
  Huanan Computer Corp.
  Guangzhou Electronic Computer Factory

Hebei Province
  Huabei Terminal Equipment Corp.
  Beidaihe #1 Radio Factory

Heilongjiang  Province
  Harbin # 3 Radio Factory
  Harbin # 4 Radio Factory

Jiamusu Electronic Factory

Henan Province
Luoyang #2 Radio Factory

Hubei Province
Hubei Radio Factory
Yangtze River Industries Factory
Yichang Semiconductors Factory

Hunan Province
Hunan Radio Factory
Hunan Electronics Research Institute Factory
Hunan Computer Factory
Shaoguang Electron Device Works
Changsha Digital Technology Lab. Equipment Factory
Changsha Microcomputer Factory
Hunan Computer Software Development Corp.
Shaoyang Radio Factory
Zhuzhou Electronic Research Institute

Jiangsu Province
Suzhou Electronic Computer Factory
Changzhou #2 Radio Factory
Jiangsu Radio Factory
Nanjing United Radio Factory
Nanjing Front Factory
Suzhou Senli Radio Factory
Changzhou Electronics Instrument Factory
Nanjing Factory #734
Jiangsu Electronic Instrument Factory
Jiangsu Computer Center
Wuxi Jiangnear Radio Equipment Plant
Shengai (Suzhou) Radio Works
Wuxi Computer Factory
Nanjing Electronics Factory
Nantong Computer Factory
Yangzhou Electronic Factory
Hongze Electronic Equipment Factory

Jiangxi Province
Ji'an Radio Module Factory

Liaoning Province
Dalian #7 Radio Factory
Liaoning Jinzhou Computer Factory
Shenyang #6 Radio Factory

Jinzhou Computer Factory
Fushun Electronic Instrument Factory
Fushun Radio Factory

National Organizations
China Computer Technical Service  Corp.
Yanshan Computer Center
China Computer Systems Engineering Corp.

Nei Mongol Autonomous Region
Hohot Electronics Equipment Co.
Hohot Electronic Equipment Factory

Shandong Province
Qingdao Microelectronic Machine Factory
Weifang Computer Factory
Shandong Electronic Equipment Factory
Zibo #4 Radio Factory
Yantai #1 Radio Factory
Yantai #2 Radio Factory
Yantai #3 Radio Factory
Yantai #6 Radio Factory
Tianshan Instrument Machine Tool  Factory

Shanghai Factories
Shanghai Computer Corp.
Shanghai Changjiang Computer Corp.
Shanghai Computer Factory (formerly # 13 Factory)
Shanghai Component Factory #5
Shanghai #5 Semi Conductor Factory
Shanghai Chongxing Electronics Corp.
Shanghai Hongyu Electronics Equipment  Corp.
Shanghai #4 Electronic Equipment  Corp.
Shanghai Yaguang Radio Factory
Shanghai #14 Radio Factory
Shanghai Relay Plant
Shanghai Huangpu Instrument Factory
Huangpu Computer Corp.

Shaanxi Province
Xian Computer Factory
Lishan (Xian) Electronics Corp.

Shanxi Province
Hubei Terminal Corp. (Yangchen)

Tianjin Factories
  Tianjin Computer Factory
  Tianjin #2 Radio FactoryTianjin #5 Radio Factory
  Tianjin Jinhua Radio Factory
  Tianjin Qinghua Radio Factory
  Tianjin Automation Instrument Factory
  Tianjin Electronic Instrument Factory
  Tianjin Hongxing Factory
  Tianjin Red Star Factory

Yunan Province
  Yunan Electronic Equipment Factory

Zhejiang Province
  Yangzhou Computer Peripheral Factory
  Hangzhou Memory Equipment Factory

Numbered Factories
  84; 602; 633; 690; 733; 750; 785; 830;  4131; 4291;  4292; 4500;
  4507; 4509; 8271;  8460

APPENDIX B

Selected List of Joint Ventures and Other Agreements

| | |
|---|---|
| Japan. Sharp Corp., LSI Plant Inquiry | 1/79 |
| France. Executed Protocol Calls for | 3/79 |

    Establishment of a computer plant (turnkey)
    NOTE: No legal framework existed for joint
    venture at this time, however in 9/79 China
    agreed to 100% foreign owned business and
    establishes China InternationalTrust and
    Development Corp.

Japan. Toshiba gets COCOM approval for sale    6-9/79
    of IC production plant in Wuxi

Japan. Sord Computer Systems plans with    2/80
    Tianjin Municipal Govt. an assembly plant in
    the Red Star plant in Tianjin

Japan. Unicom Automation Co. of Tokyo    3/80
    establishes a technology exchange committee
    with Tianjin Computer S&T Instrument Co.
    for production of micros, software, etc.

US. Sperry Univac signed a cooperation    3/80
    contract with SACI for computer assembly

Japan. Fujitsu & Tianjin Municipal S & T    4/80
    Commission explore a joint venture to develop
    a Chinese hardware/software computer system

US. Sperry Univac    4/80
    (A) An 1100/10 computer is to be used for a
    cooperative development of software
    (B) A cooperative agreement to develop a
    strong computer manufacture in China

US. Honeywell executed a cooperative agreement    7/80
    to transfer the manufacture of software to and
    to give training at the Beijing Wire Plant that
    specializes in computers and switch gear.
    The plan also involves production of large
    scale digitals and minis.

France. Thompson CSF sold a factory to China    7/80
    for manufacture of minis.

US. Ohio Micro and Yangtze River Industries    8/80
    enter into a joint venture for production
    manufacture and assembly of a C3
    microprocessor.

US. Secretary of Defense Perry announced a    9/80
    joint venture involving an IBM machine under
    supervision by Western Geophysical in China in
    return for Chinese metals for US aircraft

US. Tandy Corp. andShenyang Institute of Computer     12/80
Technology CAS, agrees to a joint venture to
assemble TRS 80's.

US. Dresser Atlas negotiated a $2 billion     12/80
contract to establish sophisticated data processing
centers to support offshore drilling

France. China contracted for     1/81
(A) the purchase of a license to produce micros
with Logabox
(B) the manufacture of computers by Thompson
CSF
(C) the purchase of a license to produce LX200
Logabox printers at the Nanjing Telecommunications
factory

France. Sems, a CSF subsidiary executed an     3/81
agreement to build a plant to assemble and test its
line of small Solar computers.

US. Wang and China agree to a joint venture     4/81
in Nanjing to produce small computers. First year
goal is $4-5 million production

Germany. Olympia Werke, a subsidiary of AEG     5/81
Telefunken executed an agreement to deliver
1000 1011 processors and production know how.

Japan. Tokai Bank and Bank of China enter an     6/81
agreement for Tokai to supply a training program
for technicians, and computer utilization know how.

Japan. Fujitsu and ISTMMB sign an agreement     9/81
for Fujitsu to provide technology on numerical
control.

US. R. C. Sanders executed an agreement to     10/81
develop and manufacture Chinese character
printers for export to Sanders

Japan. Hitachi and Beijing Teachers University     10/81
will start joint research to develop a high
performance Chinese character processing system.

US. Hewlitt-Packard and 4th MMB create a     11/81
distributorship in Beijing for the sale and service
of HP equipment.The distributorship will be
within CEIEC

US. Honeywell and Beijing Automation Industry     12/81
Corp.execute an agreement on building
management software systems.

West Germany. The Federal Republic and the     12/81
1st MMB agree to a joint venture involving
installations of process controls in Chinese
factories starting with a tool plant in Shenyang

US. Isotronix, Anchron Computer Products,     1/82

China Trade Corp., and China Corp. for
Shipbuilding Industry agree to two joint ventures
(A) establishment of a plant to manufacture printed
circuit boards
(B) production of computer components and
sub-assemblies in the CCSI facility for shipment
to Anchron

West Germany. West German Society for     1/82
Mathematics and Data Processing signed a
cooperative agreement with CAS for exchange
of data processing experts as well as joint venture
research into software technology, data bank
management systems, and telecom services.

Japan. Japan Computer Engineering and the     2/82
Chinese Desk Computer and Calculation Corp.
will undertake joint design of programs.

Australia. Melbourne University professor and     5/82
Guangdong's China Electrical Systems
Engineering Co. agree to development and
manufacture of Sinotronic CS4000 word
processors.

West Germany. Sinotype Systems Ltd., China     5/82
National Technical Import Corp., China National
Instrument Corp., Sun Hung Kai and Olympia
Werke, West Germany execute a joint venture to
sell new Chinese character processing system

France. Agreement executed with Huanan South     5/82
China Computer to import technology and
equipment to produce SEMS Solar 16 family minis

Hong Kong. Beijing Computer Industry Corp.,     8/82
the Beijing branch of CEIEC and two Hong Kong
firms agree to a joint venture to introduce Chinese
computer products to the world market and to train
Chinese

US. Several Chinese corporations executed an     8/82
agreement with the Essex Group Inc. a subsidiary
of United Technologies Inc. to transfer technology
for the manufacture of telephone cables.
Production will be at the Chengdu Cable Plant.

Japan. China Computer Technology Service Corp.     9/82
and Nippon Electric establish a Sino Japanese
software center in Beijing

US. National Semiconductor Corp. has proposed     9/82
a semiconductor manufacturing agreement

Norway. Computer Center, Trondheim Univ. and     1/83
Norsk Data A/S begin establishing a software
center in Beijing under UN auspices.

US. Sperry Corp. and China Computer Technical      5/83
Service Corp. opened a joint technological center
to provide consulting services and contract out
for software development.

Japan. Fuji Electric Co., Chugai Boeki Co. and Koyd
Trading Co. (Japan) and China Electronics
Import/ Export Corp., and Tianjin #3 semi
conductor plant sign agreement

Japan. International Scientific (Japan) and      7/83
China Aviation Equipment Co. signed an
agreement for supply of equipment and know
how for construction of PC and semi conductor
factories for $41 million.

Hong Kong. Swire Engineering Ltd. and Minong      8/83
Development Corp.of New Technology,
Fujian agree to assemble micros

United Kingdom. Sinclair Research and South      10/83
China Computer Corp.and CEIEC agree to
assemble home computers

Hong Kong. Kong Wa Electronic Enterprises      11/83
Ltd. and Guangming Overseas Chinese
Electronics Industry Co. (Shenzen) agree to
produce computer telephones.

US IBM and 1st Ministry of Machine Building      10/83
discuss a computer applications joint venture.

US. Micro Air Systems and China National      11/83
Electronics Import/Export Corp. negotiate
production of semi conductor manufacturing
equipment.

Japan. Tokyo Maruichi Shoji Co. Ltd. and      2/84
Beijing branch of CCTSC agree to produce
software packages in accordance with Japanese
standards.

US. International Software Systems Inc. and      1/84
World Info Systems Enterprises and China
Software Technology Development Center signed
a memo of understanding to act as exclusive agent
for computer hardware and establish a computer
software development training school.

US. Wang and Hubei Radio Factory set up a      3/84
cooperation and development center to develop
Chinese language computers and office automation
systems

US. Hewlitt-Packard and CEIEC sign a 10 year      4/84
agreement to establish China Hewlitt Packard Ltd.
in Beijing to manufacture computers etc.

Singapore. Lityan Development Co. and      5/84

Guangzhou Audio and Electric Appliance Factory
establish a Lityan Microcomputer Co.

US. Computerland Corp. and MMI sign letter of     5/84
intent to establish Computerland in China to sell
micros

Hong Kong. Runhai Electronics Co. and Linfen     6/84
Electronic Equipment Factory Shanxi agree to
produce computers, etc.

Hong Kong. NA, Hangzhou Automation Research     6/84
Institute and Zhejiang Provincial International
Trust and Investment Corp. establish Hangzhou
Computers Ltd.to produce Chinese character
micros and provide service

US. Applied Materials Inc. and MMI agree to     6/84
jointly operate the Applied Materials China
Service Center Beijing to install and service
semi conductor systems.

Japan. KC Ltd. and CCTSC Beijing agree to     7/84
develop software including Chinese character
software and other application software for mini
and micro systems in Kobe Japan

US. Compac and Beijing Electronic Display     8/84
Unit factory have started a computer production
operation.

US. Eastern Computers Inc. and China Henan     9/84
International Economic Technical Cooperation
Corp. established an agreement to supply
technology, circuit boards and software to
implement a Chinese character input coding
method.

US. Burroughs Corp., Yunnan Province Import     1/85
Export Corp., the Yunnan Electronic
Equipment Factory and Everbright Industrial
Corp. will assemble and distribute B20 & B25
model micros.

US. Wang Labs Inc. signed three joint venture     1/85
agreements for manufacture of computer
equipment and software, build Wang PC's with
Chinese character capability in Shanghai and
assemble Wang PC's in Xiamen.

US, Honeywell Great Wall Industrial Co.     2/85
and Beijing Data Equipment Institute establish
a computer distribution contract.

Japan. IBS Comsery Corp. and China State     9/84
Shipbuilding Corp. signed an agreement to
develop software to handle Chinese characters.

US. Sperry, CITIC , China Computer Technical     10/84

- Services Corp.and Wuxi Computer Factory agreed to manufacture and make Sperry's Mapper software system.

Japan. System Design and Consultant Co.                          10/84
and Beijing Computer Software Service Center
jointly established a software company in Tokyo

US. Sun Associates and Shijiazhuang Radio                        10/84
Plant #8 established New Star Computer
International Inc. to import and sell computers,
provide service and develop new technology.

United Kingdom. Lingnan Microelectronics                         11/84
and Lingnan Microelectronics Industrial Co.
Guangdong agree to produce large integrated
circuits.

US. Genisco Computer Corp. and Hunan Computer                    11/84
Factory signed a contract to establish the Genisco
China Computer Graphics Terminal Corp. to
produce computer terminals.

US. G. E. Co., Wuxi Electrical Apparatus Co.                     11/84
Shanghai Electrical Apparatus Research Institute,
and Tianjin Electrical Drive Design and Research
Institute set up a distributorship network to offer
GE programmable controllers.

US. Corporate Data Sciences Inc. and Amalgamated                 12/84
Computer Co. Guangdong signed an agreement
to produce CDS computer technology

Canada. International Geosystems Corp.                           12/84
established a software system for a state operated
engineering corporation

France. Scribel contracts for Chinese                            1/85
character computer graphic terminal technology.

Japan. Nippon Electronics Corp. and CEIEC                        2/85
establish a production line to manufacture 16 bit
micros for a factory in Baoding Hubei.

Japan. Tokyo Electronics Co. agreed to                           2/85
produce printers for PC's at a factory in Shenyang.

New Zealand. Mr. Peng and Haikou Electronics                     8/84
Industrial Co. set up the new China Computer
Development and Trading Co. to produce computers.

Hong Kong. Luk's Industrial Co. Ltd.,                            12/84
Zhenua Electronics Industry Corp. and Shenzen
Electronics Industry  Corp. established Huata
Electronics Corp. Ltd. to make printed circuit
boards.

Macao. Nanquang Trade Corp. and Weifang                          12/84
Electronics Industry Corp. established the Sheni
Electronics Co. in Weifang to manufacture

computers.

US. Burroughs and Huafeng Industrial Corp.                           3/85
    dicuss joint production of large scale computers.

US. Data General Corp. and Tianjin Computer Co.                      3/85
    executed a distributorship for 16 and 32 bit DG.
    systems

W. Germany. BASF, Aiwa Electronics Ltd.                              5/85
    Shenzen and CNETIEC agree on technology and
    equipment to produce magnetic products

US. Apple Computer Inc., ACI Kaihin Co. Ltd.                         5/85
    agreed to sale and distribution of Apple II and
    Macintosh Plus.

Japan. Toppan Moore Engineering Institute                           3/85
    and the Ministry of Textile Industry agreed to
    establish Xijing Computer Technical Development
    Co. to sell IBM Japan PC's

Hong Kong. Yon Hoi Trading Co., Linfen                              4/85
    Electronics Equipment Factory and Bank of
    China Taiyuan branch establish Linhai Electronics
    Industry Co. Ltd. in Shaanxi to produce
    computers, etc.

Hong Kong. Chiu Kwa Electronics Ltd. and                            5/85
    Williams Electronics Eng'g. Co. and N. A.
    Dalian establish Dalian Orient Technology
    Development Co. Ltd. to produce microprocessors,
    computer technology and consulting.

Japan. Hitachi Ltd. and the Institute of RR                         5/85
    Science (Ministry of RR) agreed to jointly
    develop Chinese language micro software and
    export PC's to the Ministry.

US. Stearns Catalytic Corp. and China National
    Non-Ferrous Metals Corp. will do design
    engineering for silicon materials in Luoyang
    Henan for production of polysilicon polished
    wafers and epitaxial wafers.

Canada. International Geosystems Corp. signed                       6/85
    an agreement to supply China's mining industry
    with sophisticated computer technology.

Canada. Sydney Development Corp. and Applied                        6/85
    Software Development Center of China State
    Shipbuilding Corp. execute an agreement to
    establish a joint venture for R&D and marketing of
    computer related products and services.

US. Motorola Inc., Harris Corp. and CEIEC                           6/85
    explore a joint semi conductor manufacturing
    operation.

US. International Technical Development                              7/85

Corp. and Shanghai Communications Univ. form
Sino-US Software Development Co.

Japan.  Vachida Yoko and Computer Center CAS          7/85
will develop software for Japanese language
computers.

US.  Olivetti (US), NA (HK) and Fujian Computer        8/85
Corp.form Bailing-Olivetti Computer
Co. to manufacture micros.

US.  Industrial Automation Systems negotiated          9/85
for equity in wholly owned foreign computer
companies in exchange for providing technology
and US marketing links.

US.  Ultimate Corp. and Jiang An Equipment             5/85
Import/Export Corp. form dealership to market
Ultimate computer systems.

Australia.  Labtam International Ltd. and  CAS          10/85
form joint venture to develop 32 bit UNIX
prototype computer using Chinese and English
software.

Japan.  Fujitsu Ltd., Agricultural Bank of             8/86
China and North China Computation Technology
Lab. agree to develop software for terminals.

Japan.  Kexi Co. Ltd. and Tianjin Economic and         1/86
Technological Development Co. sign a contract
to operate Tianjin Kexi Co. Ltd. to develop and
produce computer peripherals, accessories, and
plasma cutting and holding devices.

Japan.  Intec Inc. and CAS Computer Center             6/86
conclude basic agreement to jointly develop
software.

US.  Total Technical Services Inc., Beijing            9/86
ITIC and Beijing Institute of  Aeronautics and
Astronautics sign formal agreement to establish
Technical Services Eastern to provide computer
services.

US.  Hamilton Bright Inc. and Instrimpex              10/86
open Computer Maintenance Service Station to
service US made computers, peripherals and
provide consulting.

US.  J.H.L. Research Inc. and MEI plan  two           12/86
joint ventures to produce computers and edit
and print software.

# APPENDIX C

<u>Typical Applications</u>

### <u>Agricuture.</u>

| | |
|---|---|
| Beijing Area | 4/79 |
| Crop Inventory surveys | 10/79 |
| Crop Infestation | |
| Categorization of soils | |
| Forecasting supply and demand of tractors and other farm equipment | 5/82 |

### <u>Hydrology.</u>

| | |
|---|---|
| Data processing | 9/77 |
| Automation of hydroelectric plants | 5/79 |
| Irrigation | 4/79 |
| Water conservation | 1/82 |
| Tidal prediction and analysis | 11/86 |
| Dam seepage | 11/86 |

### <u>Medical diagnosis.</u>

| | |
|---|---|
| Ultrasonic | 12/77 |
| Heart, pulmonary, liver | 5/79 |
| Automatic clinical analysis | 5/80 |
| Cancer, gastric ulcer, gall bladder, pancreas | 5/80 |
| Tomography | 11/86 |

### <u>Other Medical.</u>

| | |
|---|---|
| Medicine | 4/79 |
| Hospital management | 3/80 |
| Medical records, monitoring patients, drug dynamics | |
| Medical network | 5/80 |

<u>Weather forecasting & meteorology.</u>     3/78,4/79

<u>Industrial control</u>

| | |
|---|---|
| Railroad traffic | |
| Coal | 4/79,9/82,6/85 |
| Oil | |
| Machine | 7/79,10/82 |
| Steel | 6/85 |

Chemicals  
Textile and jet looms                7/80, 2/82  
Aluminum production            12/81,6/85  
Flour production                     12/85  
Paper                              6/85

## Management.

Financial and economic planning     4/79  
Hotel including reservations           9/80  
Airline international reservations      2/81  
Government office automation systems   6/85  
Auto spare parts inventory control      6/85

## Shipbuilding and Shipping.           12/81

Loading and unloading  
Baoshan Iron Steel complex- Shanghai  
Container processing-Tianjin          6/82  
Whampoa  
Dalian                          6/85  
Ship control                  12/81

## Petroleum Industry.

Petrochemistry                4/79  
Petroleum research           4/79  
Product storage and distribution     6/85

## Seismological Research.             4/79

## Mapping.                        9/79

## Social Studies.                   4/79

Planning, implementing and coordinating  
     nationwide computer system.  
Retrieve economic, social,  
     demographic and statistical data.

## Food Distribution.           3/80,11/81

## Power Supply and Distribution.     4/79,6/85

## Environmental Monitoring.         4/82

## Telecommunications.            6/82

| Telephone directory inquiry system | 11/86 |
|---|---|

### Design.

| Diesel locomotives | 1/83 |
|---|---|
| Language system for computer algebra | 1982 |
| Electronic circuits | 4/79 |
| Roads and bridges | 6/85 |
| IC's using CAD | 10/86 |

| Housing Construction. | 3/80 |
|---|---|

| Municipal Traffic Control. | 6/85 |
|---|---|

| National Defense. | 4/79 |
|---|---|

## APPENDIX D

<u>Selected Training Agreements</u>

Applied Devices.
    Training included in six locations with sale         1976
  of PDP 11.
IBM.
    With sale to Shenyang Blower Factory, there was     1978
    training for integration, of numerically controlled
    machine tools and CAD.
CDC.
    With sale of 172, 173 and 175 there was a three year   1978
    training and maintenance agreement.
CDC.
    With sale of Cyber 18 mini there was a training      1978
    agreement.
Sperry Univac.                               1979
    A technical cooperation agreement (called next best
    thing to a joint venture) involved sending 30 Chinese
    to a training center in Birmingham.
Burroughs.
    Wth sale of a B6810 there were training and maintenance  1979
    agreements.
Burroughs.
    With sale of a B3950, B8766 and B92 there were    1979
    training agreements.
Hewlitt-Packard.
    Sale of HP3000 Series III involved on site training   1980
  — for 30 Chinese and maintenance over a three year period.
IBM.
    Cometals sale of used IBM 130/183J involved training.  1980
IBM.
    Census transaction involved training for 50 service   1980
    engineers, 35-40 assistant engineers and hundreds
    of technicians and programmers.
Stanford Tech. Corp.
    Transaction involved training of 14 technicians.    1980
IBM.
    Lease of IBM 3033 involved a five year contract with  1980
    IBM Japan Ltd. and Western Geophysical to handle
    training of at least 18 people.
Corelabs Inc.
    Signed a contract to provide engineering software with  1982
    Science Research Institute. Initial training to be carried
    out in Beijing, later in Dallas.
Wang Labs.

Wang and Jiaotung Univ., Shanghai, hold symposium   1982
on application of computers in education and scientific
research.

International Software Systems Inc., World Info. Systems   1984
Enterprises and China Software Technology Developmental
Center establish a software development training school.

Honeywell Info. Systems Inc.and Beijing Wired   1984
Communication Plant. Set up technical training of
Chinese personnel by Honeywell for set up and
operation of testing system.

Total Technical Svcs. Inc.
Established a training program for six Chinese   1984
companies.

Burroughs Corp.,
Ever Bright Industrial Corp., Yunan Import/Export   1985
Corp.,and Yunan Electronic Eqpt. Fac. Training
programs will be set up in China and the US for
assembly and distribution of B20's and B25's.

International Memories Inc.
Training program established with sale of disk drives,   1985
technology and assembly equipment.

Honeywell H. Yamatake and China Sichuan Instrument   1986
Complex establish a 5 year training program in US,
Japan as part of a larger agreement.

Total Technical Svcs.Inc., Beijing ITIC, and Beijing   1986
Institute of Aero. and Astro. agreement covers
technical training

Hamilton Brighton Inc. and Instrimpex. Agreement   1986
includes technical consulting services and training.

IBM Japan Ltd.
With sale of IBM 370/158 to Beijing S & T University,   1982
an arrangement for 14 Chinese engineers to be trained
by Ultimate Computer Services.

JCE.
Supply of Chinese software for Japanese computers   1981
involves 3 year training of two Chinese engineers.

UN.
Under UNESCO sponsorship, university graduates   1981
obtain Data Base and COBOL training courses

KD CO. Japan, Xiamen Electronics, and Xiamen Research   1984
Institute establish a microcomputer training school in
Xiamen, Fujian Province.

NEC.
established a training center for computer engineers   1985
in Baoding, Hebei Province.

Sord Computer Corp. and CASS will build a PC training   1985
center

Cosmo 80 Co.
    Established a training program for the Shenzen       1985
    Computer Development Co.
Intec Inc. and CAS Computer Center,  Agreement to train    1986
    Chinese computer experts to jointly develop software.
NEC.
    Acoustic System 500 sale with training.           1979
Fujitsu.
    M140 sale with basic technical cooperative  agreement    1980
    covering maintenance and software development.
Unicom.
    Microprocessor sale and license agreement  led to a     1980
    joint venture and included training.
NEC/Fujitsu.
    Joint software training center  (NEC opened 1/82)     1982
Data Plotting.
    Training of 5 geophysicists from Beijing  Geologic     1981
    Survey.
Sino on Line, Chartered on Line and Chai Luk  International   1982
    Trade enter into various training arrangements related to
    computers and software.
Chiu Hwa Electronics Ltd., and Williams  Electronics     1985
    International Trade Development  CO. established a
    training service program for the new Dalian Orient
    Computer Technology Engineering Co.
Data Prep.
    Will distribute Wicat computer and training systems     1985
BASF and Shanghai Computer Corp. Agreement provides
    staff training for Chinese.
Scintrex.
    Training and engineering.                1980

131

## APPENDIX E

Selected Manpower Data

Computer Factory; formerly Shanghai Radio Factory #13
1300 specialized workers

Beijing #1 Computer Factory; formerly Telephone Equipment Factory;
built in 1957; 5000 assembly workers, engineers and administrative
persons.

Need according to Wang Xiango Jilin Deputy, Daily Report, China, FBIS
CH 9/11/80; 100,00 people needed to operate existing computers.
500,000 needed in 1990. China can only train 2000 per year.

Article covering exhibit popularizing computers in Beijing Exhibition Hall
9/81.Reported 70,000 employees in the computer industry; 8700
technicians under SACI control.

According to China's Computer Review of 11/81  and China's Business
Review, 12/81 the computer industry has 26 computer research institutes;
99 main equipment and accessory plants; 120,000 personnel;  30,000-
40,000 of whom are devoted to service; and 6,000  are programmers.

Yuan Hua Electronic Co., Guangzhou, (Electronic Weekly 1/82) 1000
employees, 300 of whom are engineers and 50% are women.

China's Growing Computer Industry;  China Reconstructs 2/82
reports China has more than 100 computer research and manufacturing
units employing more than 7000.

Computer World 2/82 reports 1000 software technicians and 1000
software developers in China.

In China, very few people are engaged in software research. The ratio
between software and hardware research is 1:10 and in foreign countries is
1.5:1. China Report; JPRS 80949, S&T #163, 6/1/82

With the formation of Sino On Line, the Beijing Computer Industry Corp.
hopes to mobilize further its 6000  workers and 500 technicians to promote
Beijing's computer industry. Daily Report, China, FBIS CH 82-150,
8/4/82

China has a computer work force of 100,000 with 20 research institutes
and 86 manufacturing plants. Daily Report, China, FBIS CH 82-205,
10/22/82

APPENDIX F

Gap Estimates

| | | |
|---|---|---|
| Computers | Nyberg Report | 1960 |
| | | 15 yrs. |
| Computer science | Tsao, Columbia Univ. | 1967 |
| | | 5 yrs. |
| Computer hardware | IEEE, Garner report | 1979 |
| | | 10+ yrs. |
| Computer memory | Technical Survey article | 1979 |
| | | 10 yrs. |
| Computer peripherals and software | Technical Survey article | 1979 |
| | | 15 yrs. |
| Computer technology | Final Review article | 1979 |
| | | 10 yrs. |
| Processor technology | Technical Survey article | 1979 |
| | | 8-10 yrs. |
| Computer science | Computing | 1980 |
| | | 10 yrs. at least. |
| Computer hardware | Machine Design | 1980 |
| | | 10 yrs. |
| Computer manufacture | Chun, Northwestern | 1980 |
| | | 10 yrs. behind West |
| Computer development | Qian, 4th MMB | 1980 |
| | | lag far behind West |
| Computer hardware and technology | Asian Survey scientists | 1980 |
| | | 15 yrs behind US |
| Computer technology | Inst.for Int'l Research | 1980-81 |
| | | 10 yrs. behind Japan |
| Micros | Information World | 1981 |
| | | 5 yrs. behind US |
| Chip production | Electronic Weekly | 1982 |
| | | 5-10 yrs. behind West |
| Semiconductors | Integrated Engineering Co. | 1982 |
| | | 10 yrs. |
| Computer technology | China Business Review | 1983 |
| | | 10 yrs. behind US |
| Software | China Business Review | 1983 |
| | | 20 yrs. behind US |
| Fabrication and testing | China Business Review | 1983 |
| | | 25 yrs. behind US |
| Processing speed and technology | Nat'l Academy of Sciences | 1982 |
| | | 10 yrs. behind US |
| Software & peripherals | Nat'l Academy of Sciences | 1982 |
| | | 15 yrs. behind US |

APPENDIX G

<u>Typical Domestic Machines</u>

August 1      1958, 2000 cps tube type based on Soviet Ural 2. (39)

ACS 8600      16 bit 512K RAM, floppy and hard disk, CPM-85, UNIX, Basic, Cobol, Fortran, Pascal, built by Suzhou Electronic Computer Plant (168)

BCM 2      Micro, based on Zilog 80 chip; built by Beijing #2 computer factory (96)

BCM 3      Micro, built by Beijing Institute of Electronic Computer Technology (68)

C 2      1965, 32 bit, 8K memory, 25 kips; designed by East China Research Institute of Computer Technology, and South China Institute of Technology. (31,39)

CJ 709      1971, 48 bit, 32 k memory, 110 kips; compares to PDP 11/30, South China Institute of Computer Technology; Harbin Institute of Technology. (30,31,96)

CJ 1001      32 bit, 500 kips. Built by Shanghai Changjiang Computer Factory. (96)

CK 710      Built by Tianjin Automatic Instrument and Meter Plant for industrial control. (98)

CMC 80      8k read/write static memory, 8k EPROM using Z80 chip. Joint developers; Zhuzhou Electronics Research Institute and Hong Kong Jinshan Company. (99)

CS 85      Micro, using Intel 8085, 8155, and 8185 chips. User; Shanghai Research Institute of Physiology, CAS. (100,101)

DISI 142      Mini, jointly developed by Jinzhou Electric Computer Plant, Qinghua University, and 2nd branch of Beijing Institute of Technology.

DJM 330      Digital analog. User; Semiconducter Research Institute, CAS. (96)

DJS1      1958, 2K memory, 1800 ops; built by Beijing Wire Factory. Also identified as 103. (31,39,55)

| | |
|---|---|
| DJS2 | 1959, 4K memory, 10 kips; built by Beijing Wire Factory. Possibly also identified as 104. (31,39,55) |
| DJS6 | 1966, 48 bit, 32K memory, 100 kips. Built by 783 Factory, Hunan Radio Factory, and Harbin #3 Radio Factory. Possibly also identified as 108B. (31,39,55,102) |
| DJS6C | 48 bit, 32K memory (MOS) 200 kflops. Built by Beijing Wire Factory Plant 738, reporting to Ministry of Electronics Industry. (103) |
| DJS7 | 1966, 32K memory, 3000 ips. (31,39) |
| DJS8 | 8 bit, 130K memory; at Beijing Institute of Aerodynamics. (30) |
| DJS11 | 1972, 48 bit, 128K memory, 1 mips, integrated circuit, designed by East China Research Institute of Computer Technology and built by Shanghai Computer Factory. Also identified as TQ6, or 655, or 150. (39,55) |
| DJS14 | at Jiaotung University , Xian. (104) |
| DJS17 | 1972, 24 bit , 8K memory, 100 kips. Built by Beijing Wire Factory and Shanghai Radio Factory. (31,39,105) |
| DJS18 | 1974, 48 bit, 64K memory, 150 kips. Built by Jiamusu Electronic Instrument Factory and Zibo (Shandong) Radio Factory. Installed at Beijing University Computer Center. (31,39,96,105) |
| DJS19 | 12 bit, 200 kips, built by Beijing Computer Factory. (96) |
| DJS21 | 1966, 4K memory, 60 kips, transistorized. Installed at Chungshan University. (31,39,55,105) |
| DJS22 | 16 bit, 100 kips, built by Xian Computer Factory. (96) |
| DJS24 & 25 | 8K-32K RAM, 12K-96K ROM, A/D converter, built by 734 Factory. (96) |
| DJS035 | Micro built by 734 Factory. (96) |
| DJS045 | Micro built by 735 Factory. Based on Rockwell AIM65. (96) |
| DJS050 | 1977, micro, 8 bit, built by Anhui Radio Works (Hefei) |

using Motorola 7800 chips. Installed at Qinghua University. (39,55,105)

**DJS051BC**  Micro, 8 bit, 4-6K RAM, 2K EPROM. Built by Shanghai Changjiang Radio Factory. (96)

**DJS052**  8 bit, 8-48K RAM, 2-16K EPROM. Built by Anhui Radio Factory and Jiangsu Radio Factory. ( DJS052-1 has Intel 8080A chip with 1k RAM and 1K EPROM) (55,96)

**DJS053**  installed at Jiaotung University, Shanghai. (2)

**DJS054**  8 bit, 8-64K RAM, 2-4K EPROM, using Intel 8080A chip. Built by Shanghai Radio Factory. (96,107)

**DJS060**  Micro, 8 bit, using Zilog 80 chip. Built by #6 Instrument Factory and #4500 Factory. (96)

**DJS061**  Micro, 8 bit, 2-8K RAM, 2-8K ROM. Built by #1447 Institute. (96)

**DJS062**  Micro, 8 bit, 8-64K RAM, 1K ROM, 1K EPROM. Built by Hunan Radio Factory. (96)

**DJS063**  8 bit. Designed by Shaanxi Electronics Institute. (96)

**DJS064**  Micro, 8 bit, 11-64K RAM, 7K ROM. Designed by #6 Institute and built by #4500 Factory. (96)

**DJS101**  16 bit, 400 kips. (96)

**DJS108**  Installed at Jiaotung University, Shanghai. (2)

**DJS110**  1977, 16 bit, 90 kips. Built by Changzhou #2 Radio Factory.(55,96)

**DJS111**  1971. Designed and built by the Institute of Computing Technology, CAS. (104)

**DJS112**  16 bit, 150 kips. Built by Changzhou Radio Factory and Shaoguang Radio Factory. (96)

**DJS120**  1976, 16 bit, 32K memory, 200 kips. Designed by South China Institute of Technology and built by Wuxi Radio Factory. (31,39)

DJS130    1974,  16 bit, 64 K memory, 500 kips. Installed at Qinghua University, South China Institute of Technology, Harbin Institute of Technology, Chengdu Institute of Telecommunications, and Fudan University. (2,24,31,39,96,105)

DJS131    1977,  16 bit, 64 K memory, 500 kips. Built by Shanghai Radio Factory and Installed at Beijing Institute of Post and Telecommunications, Shanghai Railroad Administration, Wanting Power Plant, Xinanjiang Power Plant, Nanjing General Military Hospital, Tianjin University (with 4 Polish terminals and disk drives), Nanjing Institute of Technology, Northwest Polytechnic Institute, Xian , and Zhengzhou Power Supply Bureau. (2,24,31,55,108)

DJS132    Upgraded DJS131, 16/32 bit, 8K core, 32K MOS. Built by Tianjin Radio Factory and Suzhou Computer Factory. (96)

DJS135    DJS130 with better temperature tolerance. Built by Tianjin Radio Factory and Yunnan Electric Equipment Factory. (96)

DJS140    1978,  64-128K memory, 800 kips. Designed by Qinghua University and built by Beijing #3 Computer Factory. (55,96,109)

DJS153    16 bit, 1 mips. Built by Tianjin Radio Technological Institute Factory, Suzhou Computer Factory, Weifang Computer Factory, Tianjin Electronic Instrument Factory. (13)

DJS154    1977,  16 bit, 16-32K memory, 200 kips. Built by Beijing Wire Factory, #738 Factory, Dalian Radio Factory and installed at the Gas Turbine Establishment at the Atmospheric Test Facility, (Jiangzhou), and the Graduate University, CAS. (30,31,55,96)

DJS155    1978. (39)

DJS160    1978. (39,55)

DJS180    (55)

DJS183    16 bit, 32K memory, 200 kips. Designed by North China Institute of Computer Technology and built in four configurations. Installed at Hubei Radio Factory for guided navigation equipment and at Northwest Telecommunications Engineering Institute, Xian. (23,96,104)

DJS184    16/32 bit, 500 kips. Designed by North China Institute of Computer Technology and built by #1915 Institute. (23,103,110)

DJS185    16/32 bit, 1M memory, 3 mops. Designed by North China Institute of Computer Technology and built by Shanghai Computer Factory. (23,110)

DJS186    16/32 bit, 248K memory, 1 mips, with a line printer, a typeprinter, two disk drives, and a X-Y plotter. Designed by North China Institute of Computer Technology and built by #1915 Institute. One unit installed at CAS, (32,96,103)

DJS210    1978, 16 bit, 100 kips. Designed by North China Institute of Computer Technology and built by Changzhou #2 Radio Factory. (31,39,55,96,104)

DJS220    1978, 32 bit, 128K memory, 200 kips. Designed by North China Institute of Computer Technology and built by Beijing Wire Factory, Nanjing Telecommunications Factory, Shanghai Radio Factory, and Harbin Radio Factory. (23,31,39,55,96,104)

DJS240    1978, 64 bit, 400 kips. Designed by North China Institute of Computer Technology and installed at Beijing University. (23,31,39,55,96,104)

DJS260    1978, 64 bit, 1 mips. Designed by North China Institute of Computer Technology, built by #1915 Institute and installed at Beijing University. (23,31,39)

DJS300    1978. (39,96)

DJS310    Built by Beijing #1 Computer Factory. (96)

DJS622    1976, 32K memory, 400 kips,with 10 terminals. Built and used at Northwest Polytechnic University, Xian. (2)

DZS183A    Built by Zhejian Institute of Computer Technology. (98)

EYC032A    Micro, 32K memory, 12K EPROM. Jointly developed by Guangzhou Yuanhua Electric Company and Hong

Kong Shida Electronics Company. (99)

HDS9
1979, 42 bit, 512K memory, 5 mips, integrated circuit. Designed and built by East China Research Institute of Computer Technology. (2,23,110)

HDS801
1981, 32 bit, 500 kflops integrated circuit with imported MOS memory and compatible and interchangeable Bulgarian and Chinese disk drives. Designed and built by East China Research Institute of Computer Technology. (2,96)

HN-3000
Mini built by Huanan Computer Corp., Guangzhou (158)

J501
1964, 50 kips, 8K magnetic core memory. Designed and built by East China Research Institute of Computer Technology. (2)

JD101
12 bit, 100 kips. Built by Jiamusu (Heilongjiang) Electronic Instrument Factory. (96)

JS10A
Medical computer. (25)

JS110
16 bit, 60K memory, at Shanghai Regulating Instrument Plant. (111)

JSY1
Fudan University. (39)

KD3
1975, 64K, 500 kips. Designed and built by Science and Technology University, CAS, at Hefei. (2)

MTJ16
Mini. (24)

NCI 2780
Super mini, board and software compatible with VAX 780, equipped with DEC hard disk and tape drives, developed by North China Institute of Computer Technology. (130)

RJX1
At Institute of Semiconductor Design, CAS. (39)

SJ771 & 773
16 bit, 256K memory. Developed by Shanghai Computing Research Institute. (113)

TQ1
1966, (39)

TQ3
1971, 24 bit, 8K memory, 100 kips. (39)

| | |
|---|---|
| TQ5A | 1977, 48 bit, 32K memory, 160 kips. Built by Shanghai Radio Factory. (105) |
| TQ11 | 1971, 36 bit, 18K memory, 50 kips. Built by Shanghai Radio factory #13. (31) |
| TQ15A | 1977, 48 bit, 32K memory, 160 kips. Built by Shanghai Radio Factory. (31) |
| TQ16 | 1975, 48 bit, 392 K memory, 200 kips. Designed by East China Research Institute of Computer Technology and built by Shanghai Radio Factory #13. Installed at Shanghai Research Institute of Shipbuilding Technology, Hudong Shipyard, and East China Institute of Textile Science and Technology. Also identified as 709. (31,39,55,96) |
| TQ21 | 4K Office Computer, built by Shanghai Radio Factory. (105) |
| WSJ2 | 8 bit, 64K memory, 150 kips. Installed at Jiaotung University, Xian. (104) |
| X2 | 1965, 32 bit, 8K memory, 52 kips. (55,39) |
| YEE-8100 | Micro built by Yunnan Electronic Equipment Factory (158) |
| ZD 2000, 2000A | Micros built by Huabei Terminal Equipment Co. Baoding and Yanshan Computer Application Research Center (158) |
| ZXJX | Micro, manufactured by Hunan Computer Factory in Changsha, 128 K memory, Z 80 microprocessor with expanded keyboard including some 25 function keys. (130) |
| 013 | 1976, 48 bit, 120K memory, 2 mips, with two 10M disk drives. Designed by the Institute of Computing Technology and installed at the Computational Institute, CAS. (24,2,39,31,104,105,61) |
| 2D 1000 | Portable with Chinese character capability (145) |
| 2D 3100 | Picture language with Chinese character capability (145) |
| 1153 | High grade digital computer (156) |

| | |
|---|---|
| 1155-1 | Ruggedized model of the 1153 (156) |
| 1163 | Mini incorporating bi-polar, bit slice technology, 200 ns. instruction cycle, built by Jinzhou Electronic Computer Factory (174) |
| 061 | Mini, built by #1447 Institute in Shenyang. (110) |
| 77 | 16 bit, designed as language oriented micro by Shaanxi Institute of Microcomputers. (111) |
| 109B | 1965, 32 bit, 32 K memory, 120 kips. Developed and built by the Institute of Computing Technology, CAS. (23) |
| 109C | 1967, 48 bit, 32 K memory, 180 kips, transistorized machine. Designed by North China Institute of Computer Technology. (23,31) |
| 111 | 1971, 48 bit, 32 K memory, 180 kips. Designed by North China Institute of Computer Technology and installed at the Research Institute of Computing, CAS. (23,100,31) |
| 150AP | A DJS11, modified for vector processing, 1.4 mips, 24 bit, 72K memory. Developed by the Institute of Computing Technology, CAS and installed at the Ministry of Petroleum. (61) |
| 151-3 | Large frame, 1.3 mips with 64 bit, and 2.5 mips with 32 bit. (112) |
| 151-4 | Large frame, 2.4 mips with 64 bit, and 4.0 mips with 32 bit. (112) |
| 441B3 | 1968, 24 bit, 256K memory, 70 kips. Built at Tianjin University and installed at South China Institute of Technology , Tianjin University and the Municipal Commission of S&T, Tianjin. (2,39,31) |
| 702 | 1974, 24 bit, 8K memory, 100 kips (39) |
| 719 | 1973, 48 bit, 32K memory,125 kips, with Algol 60 compiler. Designed by Fudan University. (31) |
| 757 | IC machine, 64 bit, 4M memory, 10 mips. Developed and built by the Institute of Computing Technology CAS. (61) |

801 — 1981, medium scale , 500K ops, imported MOS memory, developed be East China Research  Institute of Computer Technology. (2)

1001 — 1976, 500 kips integrated circuit machine with six vertical drive 325mm magnetic disks. Built by East China Research Institute of Computer Technology. (2)

8030 — Supermini, board compatible with IBM  370/138, developed and built by East China  Research Institute of Computer Technology. (130)

East Sea — Micro, 0520C compatible with IBM PC XT, 16 bit, 256K memory, SCCDOS (Dong Hai) Developed by Shanghai Electronic Computer Factory and built by Beijing Computer Factory #3.(130)

Galaxy — 100 mips, equipped with domestically built  X1 preprocessor and F1 simulator developed by the Changsha Institute of Technology at Changsha. (130)

Golden Purpose — Micro, with an 8 bit microprocessor,  Apple II E look alike manufactured by  Factory #9 in Nanjing. (130)

Great Wall — 0520 , 0530A  & 386 micros, 16 bit, color  capability, CCDOS, developed by the Beijing  Research Institute Computer System Engineering reported to be comparable to IBM PC XT & AT. (130)

MCF — Micro, comparable to Apple II,  8 bit  Motorola 808A microprocessor, 128 K memory,  built by Changsha Microcomputer Factory. (130)

Purple Mountain — Micro, comparable to Apple II,  manufactured by Nanjing Telephone Exchange  #734. (130)

Xinghe II — Micro built by #8 Radio Factory, Foshan (158)

Yueling — Micro built by Weifang Computer Co. (158)

Zijin II — Micro built by Zijin Information Industry  Corp. Nanjing (158)

APPENDIX H

Typical Computers Imported by China

UNITED STATES
Alpha Micro, one at the Science and Technology University, CAS, Hefei, and one at Jiaotung University, Shanghai. (2)

Altos 3068 Systems (two) for office management at Beijing Olympic Hotel.

Apple II, at Quinghua University; research on speech recognition. (104)

Apollo DN660 CAD system at Shanghai Institute of Computing Technology. (130)

Aydin 5216 color display system for research on process control. (110)

Burroughs
1955 at Jiaotung University, Shanghai. (2)

B3950, B876 with 35MT600 data entry.

Three small scale machines at the Beijing Institue of Foreign Trade for training in basic accounting and import/export contract management. (110)

B6810 with 16 display terminals furnished by UNDP and installed at the Beijing Center for International Economic Information. (22,110)

B7700 to CAS in 1976.(170)

B7830 for Huafeng Industry Corporation. (96)

Network including computer capable of 2.5 mops, four smaller computers, six batch processing terminals and 78 other terminals at Huafeng Industry Corp. in Beijing.(159)

Control Data Corporation
Jiaotung University, Shanghai. (2)

Cyber 172 at the Research Institute of Computing, CAS. (100)

Cyber 180-845 and 180-155 imported for installation at Zhongyuan oil field and Daqing oil field. (147)

CDC 720's. Nine or twelve at installations of the Ministry of Petroleum, for geophysical exploration; four at Zhouxian, two at Beijing, two at Urumqui and two at Guanxi Province. (22,110)

CDC 730 to the China National Oil and Gas Exploration and Development Corporation for geophysical exploration at the Daqing oilfield. (110)

CDC 750 for Geophysical exploration. (12)

Commodore
Approximately 50 micros. (96)

Computervision
Two CAD systems for watch and printed circuit board manufacturer in Xian. (96) One system for oil piping design at Yan Shan Petrochemical Works.(96)

Cromemco
Eight micros at Beijing University. (2) Ten micros at Tianjin University. (2) Four micros at Northwestern Polytechnic University, Xian. (2) One micro at Jiaotung Univesity, Xian (2) Four micros at Northwestern Telecommunications Engineering Institute, Xian, (104) One micro at Luoyang Bearing Plant. (114). One micro at Hunan University. (114) One micro at the East China Institute of Textile Science and Technology for information retrieval. (114) One micro at Qinghua University. (2) One micro at Lyoyang Tractor Research Institute. (114) One micro at the Hunan Computer Center for Chinese Character Coding. (105)

Data General
Two Eclipse 16 bit S/140s, at the Great Wall Hotel, Beijing, for hotel account managing.(183)

Digital Equipment Corporation
VT100 at Jiaotung University, Xian. (2)

Six 11/03s at Quinghua University. (104)

Two 11/03s at Beijing University. (2)

One PDP 11/04 controlling a fatigue tester.(30)

One PDP 11/23 at Tianjin University, (2) one at the China Software Technique Corp., one at the Institute of Automation CAS, at Shenyang and one at the Anhui Computer Center. (130)

Five PDP 11/24s four at Chengdu Institute of Radio Engineering and one at the Institute of Optics and Electronics, CAS, Chengdu (130)

PDP 11/30 at Quinghua University. (2)

Four PDP 11/34s, one at Fudan University, (2) three at CAS Inst.of Computing Technology. (130)

Six PDP 11/45s for oil exploration. (110)

Two PDP 11/60s at the Institute of Computer Technology, CAS. (104)

One PDP 11/70 at Northwest Telecommunications Institute at Xian.(110)

One machine at Chengdu Telecommunications Institute.

VAX 11/750 at Hefei University of Science and Technology. (130)

VAX 785 at CAS Institute of Computer Technology for CAD work.(130)

Three VAX 11/780s at Northwest Polytechnic University, Xian , Chengdu Institute of Radio Engineering (130) and Zhejiang University.(181)

Electronic Associates
One 700 Hybrid at Harbin Engineering Institute for dynamic system research. (110)

Gould
32/2750 at Hefei University of Science and Technology. (130)

Hewlitt Packard
One HP 1000 at Tianjin University for research in electrical engineering. (2)

One HP 1000 at the Institute of Thermophysics, CAS, for

data acquisition and reduction.

One HP 1000 at the Institute of Automation CAS, at Shenyang. (130)

Five HP 3000 Series III at the Center for International Cooperation in Beijing provided by UNDP. (12,110)

Fifty HP 9800 micros.

9845B at Institute of Optics and Electronics, CAS, Chengdu. (130)

Honeywell
180 DPS-6 minis at various locations including Wageng University, The People's University, National University of Defense Technology and the University of South China and China Travel Service. (12,130,161)

Seventeen DPS-8s at key universities including Jiaotung University, Xian, Fudan University, Hefei University of Science and Technology, Tianjin University (130), Beijing Wired Commuications Plant and other installations. (161)

Hughes
Micro at the Academy of Electron Technology, Ministry of Electronic Industry.

IBM
One 370/138 at the Shenyang Blower Works for process control. (110)

Three 370/148s one at East China Research Institute of Computer Technology and two at Shanghai Institute of Computing Technology.(130)

One 370/158 at the Chengdu Computer Applications Institute. (115)

One 3031 at Dalian shipyard. (130)

One 3032 with 370 terminals at the Hong Kong branch of the Bank of China. (116)

One 3033 owned by Western Geophysical for oil exploration in China.(110, 12)

Twenty 4331 machines for demographics. (2,128)

One 4331 at CAS Computer Center.

Twenty-one 4300 series. (128)

Five 4341s, one for ship design at Shanghai Shipping Corporation, (110,117) one at CAS Computer Center. (130)

4361 at Sichuan Provincial Computer Center, Chengdu. (130)

IBM PCs at Jiaotung University, Shanghai, (2) CAS Inst. of Computer Technology, China Software Technique Corp., Northeast Polytechnic Institute, the Hunan Provincial Computer Center. (130).

5550 at Jiaotung University, Xian. (130)

Nova 1200. (31)

Perkin Elmer
XL40 at Beijing Computer Center furnished by UNDP. (110)

Five 3220s for China National Oil and Gas Exploration and Development Corporation. (12)

Prime
Four 550s, at China Tourist Bureau, (118) Jiaotung University, Xian (2) Shijiazhuang in Hubei Province for uranium exploration, (110) Yellow River flood control and water management. (12)

One 650 at Beijing Institute of Aeronautics and Astronautics. (30)

One 750 at China Petroleum Planning and Engineering Institute, Beijing. (184)

Radio Shack
TRS 80s at Hangzhou Special Radio Plant (114) Graduate University, CAS (2) Science and Technology University, Hefei, CAS (2) Institute of Artificial Intelligence, Hefei, (CAS) Jiaotung University, Shanghai. (2)

Sperry Univac
    One machine at Institute of Thermophysics, CAS (2) Three
    1100/10s at Semiconductor Institute, CAS (2) Beijing
    Science & Technology University (119)
    Document Service Center. (120)

    Two 1100/11s at Research Institute of Petroleum
    Processing. (119,121)

    One 1100/12 for the State Seismological Bureau. (122)

    One 1100/60 at the Beijing Document Center. (12)

Televideo
    11 micros at Northeast Polytechnic Institute, Shenyang.
    (130)

Wang
    Eight VS2200/E16s, two VS80s  at Beijing Municipal
    Computer Center (130) Tianjin Inst. of Scientific and
    Technical Information. (130)

AI Electronics
    Two AICOM C5 minis at Nankai Fish Institute, Guangzhou
    (110) Tokai Fish Institute, Shanghai. (110)

    Twenty-three AI M16s for universities provided from funds
    from World Bank.

Fujitsu
    Two FACOM M140s at University of Science and
    Technology, Hefei, CAS (2) China Ocean Shipping
    Company, Shanghai. (123)

    One FACOM M150 at Qinghua University. (2)

    One FACOM M160 at the Municipal Commission of Science
    and Technology, Tianjin. (2)

Hitachi
    Twenty-one L320 office computers. (110)

    Eleven HITA M 150's for use in import/export trade. (110)

    One 150 at Hunan Provincial Computer Center. (130)

    Two M160s for geological research. (110)

One M170 for a meteorological observation station in Beijing. (110)

One R330 at CAS Computer Center.

One L340 at CAS Computer Center.

Mitsubishi
One 256K CPU at White Swan Lake Hotel, Guangzhou. (124)

Nippon Electric
One machine at China Technical Service Corp. (96)

Two ACOS 300s at Beijing Service Center for software development (2) Shanghai for inventory control.(110)

One ACOS 500 at the Ministry of Post and Telecommunications.(122)

One ACOS 400 at Northeast Polytechnic Institute, Shenyang. (130)

Victor Sorax
One unit at Jiaotung University, Shanghai.(2)

Webster Micro
Three Spectrum units at Beijing Institute of Technology.(96)

Elliot 803 at the Medical Research Institute.(102)

Arch 1000 for process control.(102)

Scintrex for geophysical data interpertation.(125)

Honeywell Bull
HIS 61/60 for teleprocessing at People's Bank of China. (102,110)

Two IRIS 50s for Petrochemical research and Beijing Institute of Aeronautics.(102,110)

SEMS MITRA 125 at Yan Liang Flight Test Research Institute.(30)

SETI PALLAS at Nanjing University.(110)

Dietz 621 for production control and management, Wuhan Steel
Corp. (107)

Siemens
4004 for process control, Hangzhou Turbine Works.

7760 in Xian.(30)

Norsk Data ND 500(126)

Two Felix C512s
Beijing Institute of Post and Telecommunications ; Institute
of Mathematics, Beijing, CAS.

Two Felix C256s at
Northwest Polytechnic University, Xian (2)
Beijing Institute of Aeronautics & Astronautics.(30)

# VII. INDEX